FOOT MEASURING ADVICE

1. Place the measuring size chart on the floor and put your foot on it. Place the heel on the mark shown on the chart and stand straight.

2. Use a pen to r point of your put the pen the size char

3. Check the m chart and yo EU and UK s

WOMEN'S
SIZE CHART

▶

Heel Here

MEN'S
SIZE CHART

▶

Heel Here

SHOE DESIGN

A HANDBOOK FOR
FOOTWEAR DESIGNERS

FASHIONARY

First Edition: Jun 2015
First Edition (Revised): Nov 2015
Second Edition: Sep 2016

ISBN 978-988-13547-1-6
SN SDBv12160912PBCB

Designed and published by Fashionary International Ltd
Manufactured in China

Project Management by Penter Yip & Mia Cheung.

Thanks to everyone who gave us feedback & suggestions.

Credit to the contributors to this project:
Mia Cheung, Zoe Kwok, Vikki Yau, Charlene Wong, Karmuel Young, Ginny Chan,
Grace Hung, Ian Fieggen, Sevara Mirkhusanova, Iskender Asanaliev, Ho Ho Tak, Vita
Yang, Travis Li, Anna Battista, Man Ho & Angus, Monique So

Fashionary Shoes Design is an ongoing project, if you have any feedback, please
don't hesitate to send it to feedback@fashionary.org.

@fashionary
@fashionarybook
@fashionary
@fashionary

Fashionary Team
Sep 2016

CONTENTS

LIBRARY

DETAIL LIBRARY

TOE TYPES

 Pointed

 Almond

 Oblique

 Narrow Round/ U-throat

 Round Square

 Square Toe

Wide Round

 Balloon

Round

 Egg

 Shell

 Wide Square/ A-line

 Wide Overcurve

Sweetheart/ Lip Throat

 Narrow Square/ U-throat

Long V-throat

 Medium V-throat

 Short V-throat

 Half Moon/ Narrow Overcurve

 Swirl Moccasin Tip

Medallion Tip

 Wing Tip

Moccasin Tip

 U-shaped Tip

Center Seamed Tip

Straight Tip

 Peep

Keyhole

 Plain Toe

Apron Toe / Moe Toe

 Bicycle Toe

 Cap Toe

Perf Toe

Split Toe

 Wing Tie

HEEL TYPES

 Flat Heel

 Pinafore Heel

 Wedge Heel

 Secret Heel

 Common Sense Heel

 Spanish Heel

 Military Heel

 Cuban Heel

 Set Back Heel

 Dutch Heel

 Comma Heel

 Louis/Flared Heel

 Flange Heel

 Stacked Heel

 Diamond Heel

 Square Heel

Barrel Heel

Kitten Heel

French Heel

Cone Heel

Spool Heel

 Continental Heel

 Pin Heel

 Chunky Heel

 Boulevard Heel

Stiletto Heel

SHOE LIBRARY

FLATS

Ballet Flat
(refer to P.80)

Folding Ballet Flat
(refer to P.81)

Bandage Ballet Flat

Espadrille
(refer to P.82)

Slip-on
(refer to P.83)

Mary Jane Flat
(refer to P.84)

Thong

Clog
(refer to P.85)

Mule

D'Orsay Flat

Bow Shoe

Evening Slipper
(refer to P.86)

Opera

Opera Pump
(refer to P.87)

Open Shank

Boat Shoe / Deck Shoe
(refer to P.88)

Moccasin

Snaffle Moccasin

Driving Shoe

Wallabee
(refer to P.89)

Adelaide

Loafer

Slip-on Loafer
(refer to P.90)

Bit Loafer

Venetian Loafer

Penny Loafer
(refer to P.91)

Tassel Loafer
(refer to P.92)

Brogue

Blind Brogue

Quarter-Brogue

Semi-Brogue

Austerity Brogue

Buck

Oxford
(refer to P.93)

Balmoral /
Galosh Oxford

Kiltie Oxford

Saddle Oxford / Bicolor

Spectator

Desert

Derby
(refer to P.94)

Blucher
(refer to P.95)

Wingtips

Long Wing

Monkstrap

Double Monkstrap

Evening Shoe

Norwegian

Whole Cut Oxford
(refer to P.96)

SANDALS

Flipflop

Slider

Cross Thong

Cross Over Thong

Ankle Strap Sandal
(refer to P.97)

Slingback Thong
(refer to P.98)

Huarache
(refer to P.99)

Gladiator
(refer to P.100)

Fisherman Sandal

Wörishofer

Salt Water Sandal

Geta

Contoured Insole
Sandal

Flatform

Curved Sole Sandal

Cork Sandal

Mule
(refer to P.101)

Ghillie
(refer to P.102)

T-bar

Cross Over

Multi Strap

Cut-out

Strappy

Espadrille Wedge

HIGH HEEL SHOES

Pump
(refer to P.103-108)

Pointy Pump
(refer to P.109)

Mary Jane Pump
(refer to P.110)

Stiletto
(refer to P.111)

D'Orsay Pump

Slingback
(refer to P.112)

Ankle Strap

Strappy

T-bar
(refer to P.113)

Double Strap

Cross Strap

Side Cross Strap

Peep Toe
(refer to P.114)

Ghillie Pump
(refer to P.115)

Loafer Pump
(refer to P.116)

Ruby Slipper

Mule

Kiltie Pump

Platform
(refer to P.117)

Wedge
(refer to P.118)

Oxford Pump
(refer to P.119)

Spectator

Heel-less
(refer to P.120)

Lita Boot

BOOTS

Flat Shoe Boot

Ankle Boot
(refer to P.121)

Chukka
(refer to P.122)

Desert Boot

Cut-out Boot

Button Up Boot

Side Gore Boot / Chelsea
(refer to P.123)

Granny Boot

Multi Buckle Boot

Multi Strap Boot

Strapped Boot

Tassel Boot

Steel-toe Boot

Dress Boot
(refer to P.124)

Zip Up Boot

Duck Boot
(refer to P.125)

Hobnail Boot

Work Boot

Australian Boot

Hiking Boot
(refer to P.126)

Jodhpur Boot
(refer to P.127)

Combat Boot

Deck Boot

Jungle Boot

Harness Boot

Pecos Boot
(refer to P.128)

Biker Boot

Frye Boot

Logger Boot
(refer to P.129)

Paratrooper Boot

UGG Boot
(refer to P.130)

Engineer Boot

Galoshe / Wellington Boot

Touring Boot

Rigger Boot

Tanker Boot

Quilted Boot

Mukluk

Snow Boot

Valenki

Indian Boot

Hessian Boot

BOOTS (CONT'D)

Cossack Boot

Cowboy Boot
(refer to P.131)

Jockey Boot/ Riding Boot

Slouch Boot
(refer to P.132)

Knit Top Boot

Knee High Boot

ATHLETIC SHOES & SNEAKERS

Plimsoll

Mule Plimsoll

Vans Slip-on
(refer to P.133)

Low-top Converse
(refer to P.134)

High-top Converse
(refer to P.135)

Sneaker

Platform Sneaker

Skate Sneaker

Zip Up Sneaker

Bouldering Shoe

Hiking Shoe

Basic Trainer

Sling Back Trainer

Tennis Shoe

Jogging Shoe

Soccer Shoe
(refer to P.136)

Golf Shoe

Bowling Shoe
(refer to P.137)

Running Shoe
(refer to P.138)

Cycling Shoe

Wedge Trainer

Basketball Shoe
(refer to P.139)

Five Toe Shoe

Wetsuit Boot

Mountaineering Boot

Snowboard Boot

Ski Boot

Racing Boot

Motorcycle Boot

Motocross Boot

HISTORICAL SHOES

ANCIENT TIMES (BEFORE 5TH CENTURY)

Ancient Egypt
c. 1500 BC

Ancient Egypt
c. 1330-1085 BC

Ancient Egypt
c. 1330-1085 BC

Ancient Egypt
c. 1000-600 BC

Mesopotamia
Babylonian c. 500BC

Ancient Greece
c. 450 BC

Ancient Greece
c. 450-400 BC

Ancient Greece
c. 450 BC

Ancient Greece
c. 450 BC

Ancient Greece
c. 450 BC

Ancient Greece
c. 450 BC

Ancient Rome
c. 31 BC - AD 100

Ancient Rome
c. AD 100-200

Ancient Rome
Caligae muliebres

Ancient Rome
Crepida

Byzantine
c. AD 400-500

Byzantine
c. AD 550

British Celtic
c. AD 100-300

MEDIEVAL PERIOD (5TH - 15TH CENTURIES)

Byzantine
c. AD 1100

Byzantine
c. AD 1100

England
c. 1120-1140

England
c. 1300-1450

England
Poulaines

England
Trippe

England
Trippe

England
c. 1430-1440

England
15th century

France
Poulaines

France
c. 1440-1450

German
c. 1180-1199

German
c. 1430-1450

Italy
12 century

Italy
c. 1375-1399

Italy
c. 1460-1470

Men's Boot
c. 1250-1350

Men's Boot
c. 1300

RENAISSANCE PERIOD (15TH - 17TH CENTURIES)

France Bearpaw

England
c. 1520

England
c. 1500-1515

England
c. 1500-1515

England
c. 1640-1650

England
Slap Sole

RENAISSANCE PERIOD (15ᵀᴴ -17ᵀᴴ CENTURIES) (CONT'D)

Spain
c. 1540

Spain
c. 1590-1600

Venice Chopine
c. 1600

Venice Chopine

Venice Chopine

Venice Chopine

Venice
c. 1740

Italy
c. 1500-1515

Italy
c. 1500-1600

England
c. 1700-1715

England
c.1785

Persian men's shoe
17th century

AGE OF ENLIGHTENMENT (LATE 17ᵀᴴ - 19ᵀᴴ CENTURIES)

England
c. 1870

England
c. 1895

England
19th Century

England
19th Century

England
19th Century

England
19th Century

England
19th Century

Portugal
c. 1770

France
c. 1730

France
c. 1750

France
19th Century

France
19th Century

EASTERN HISTORICAL SHOES

India
Paduka

India
Mojari

Indonesia
Stilted Sandal

Korea Wooden Shoes
Na-Mok-Shin

Japan
Nikko Geta

Japan
Okobo

Japan
Imperial Boot

Japan
Falconry Boot

Japan
Tengu Geta

China Tiger-head
Kids Shoe

China Sycee Shoes
Yuan Baodi

China Three-inch
Lotus Shoe

China Pedestal
Lotus Shoe

Chian Pedestal Shoes
Hua Pandi

China Court Boot

Middle East Nalin

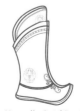
Mongolia Gutal Boot

Tibet Sombha Boot

SIGNATURE SHOES

SIGNATURE SNEAKERS

Nike Air Force 1
1986

Nike Air Max 1
1987

Nike Air Jordan XI
1995

Nike Dunk
1998

Adidas Super Star
1969

Adidas Stan Smith
1971

Adidas Top Ten
1979

Adidas X Jeremy Scott Wing
2008

Reebok Pump Fury
1994

Onitsuka Tiger
Mexico 66
1966

Vans Slip-on
1976

K-Swiss Classic
1966

Converse High-top
Chuck Taylor All Star
1917

Converse Low-top
Chuck Taylor All Star
1957

New Balance 574
1988

New Balance M992
2006

Puma Clyde
1973

Rick Owens
Sneaker

SIGNATURE DESIGNER SHOES

Rockstud
- Valentino

Dolly Pump
- Charlotte Olympia

Ruffle Shoe
- Prada

Banana Heel
- Prada

Backwards Heel
- Marc Jacobs

Minimarket

Lace Low Boot
- Dr. Martens

Buckle Pump
- Roger Vivier

Kiraro
- Celine

Jean Paul Gaultier

Alexander McQueen

Armadillo Heel
- Alexander McQueen

Lita
- Jeffrey Campbell

Night Walk
- Jeffrey Campbell

Benched
- Jeffrey Campbell

Plexi Heel
- Maison Martin Margiela

Tabi
- Maison Martin Margiela

Cage Shoe
- YSL

SIGNATURE DESIGNER SHOES (CONT'D)

Homage to Picasso
- André Perugia

Spiral Heel
- André Perugia

Homage to George Braque
- André Perugia

Heel-less
- André Perugia

Damesmuil
- André Perugia

Corkscrew Heel
- André Perugia

Beigefoldedshoe
- Marloes ten Bhömer

Rapidprototypedshoe
- Marloes ten Bhömer

Wings Variations
- Tea Petrovic

Lipstick Heel
- Alberto Guardiani

Three-heeled Pump
- ACNE

Ballet Pump
- Christian Louboutin

Deliah
- Senso

Beckett
- Isabel Marant

Stiletto Sneaker
- Cyd Jouny

Lace Platform
- Nicholas Kirkwood

Erdem
- Nicholas Kirkwood

Möbius
- United Nude

Eamz
- United Nude

Ultra Loop
- United Nude

Zaha Hadid
for United Nude

Iris Van Herpen
for United Nude

Iris Van Herpen
for United Nude

Iris Van Herpen
for United Nude

Mojito Shoes
- Julain Hakes

Zaha Hadid
for Melissa

Flamingo
- Kobi Levi

Banana
- Kobe Levi

Project 1
- Finsk

Project 2
- Finsk

Project 3
- Finsk

Alexandra
- Sebastian Errazuriz

Lady Belle
- Noritaka Tatehana

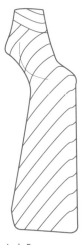
Lady Romanesque
- Noritaka Tatehana

FOOT OVERVIEW

FOOT SHAPES

Egyptian

Roman

Greek

Germanic

Celtic

Asian

ARCH SHAPES

Flat Foot

Normal

High Arch

FOOT TERMINOLOGY

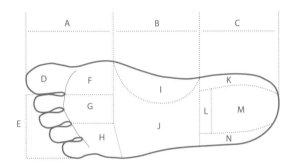
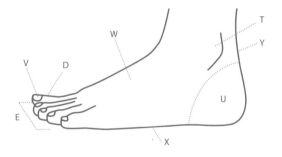
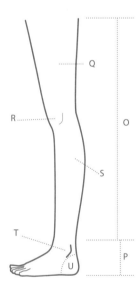

A	Forefoot
B	Midfoot
C	Heel
D	Hallux / Big Toe
E	2nd, 3rd, 4th & Little Toe
F	1st Metatarsal Head
G	2nd & 3rd Metatarsal Head
H	4th & 5th Metatarsal Head
I	Arch
J	Lateral Midfoot
K	Inner Heel
L	Heel Front
M	Heel
N	Outer Heel
O	Leg
P	Foot
Q	Thigh
R	Knee
S	Calf
T	Ankle
U	Rearfoot
V	Nail
W	Upper Side of the Foot
X	Sole of the Foot
Y	Achilles Tendon

FOOT MEASUREMENTS

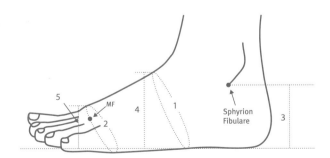
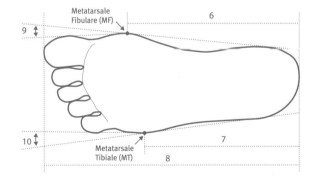

1	Instep Circumference	6	Instep Length
2	Ball Girth	7	Fibulare Instep Length
3	Sphyrion Fibulare Height	8	Foot Length
4	Instep Height	9	5th Toe Angle
5	Ball Height	10	1st Toe Angle

SHOE LAST OVERVIEW

TYPES OF SHOE LASTS

Solid Last
The solid last is used for low-heeled shoes and sandals.

Scoop Black Last
It is used for the manual shoe production. It has a wedge on the top and can be detached from the main body.

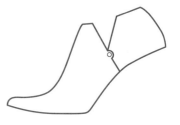

Hinge Last
A last used for all kinds of shoe productions. It can be removed from the shoe without damaging the back part of the shoe.

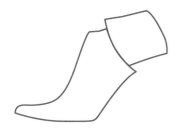

Telescopic Last
The telescopic last will slide and reduce in length when slipping.

Three-piece Last
The three-piece last was used for forced lasting boots or reversed slippers in the past. After the removal of the center and back parts, it is easier to remove the front part.

SHOE LAST ANATOMY

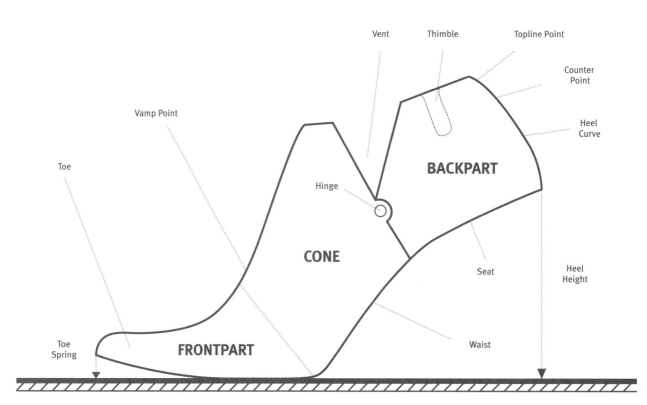

SHOE LAST MEASUREMENTS

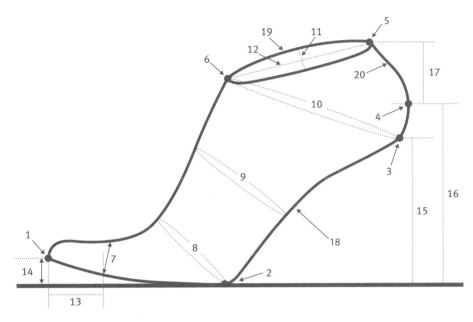

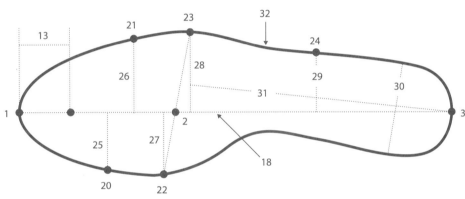

01.	Front point of the last bottom	17.	Back height
02.	Bottom support surface (tread point)	18.	Longitudinal axis of shoe last bottom (side view)
03.	Back point of the last bottom	19.	Topline
04.	Maximum point of heel curve	20.	Big toe contact point
05.	Back point of topline	21.	Little toe contact point
06.	Front point of topline	22.	The first metatarsal-phalange joint (MPJ)
07.	Toe depth	23.	The fifth metatarsal-phalange joint (MPJ)
08.	Ball girth	24.	Waist point
09.	Instep girth	25.	Inner width of the big toe
10.	Heel girth	26.	Outer width of the little toe
11.	Width of topline	27.	First metatarsal-phalange inner width
12.	Length of topline	28.	Fifth metatarsal-phalange outer width
13	Last toe allowance	29.	Outer width of waist
14.	Toe spring	30.	Width of heel area
15.	Heel elevation (heel height)	31.	Heel centre line
16.	Height of the maximum point of the heel curve and the ground plane	32.	Shoe last bottom outline (last bottom pattern)

SHOE LAST MATERIALS

	Historical	Bespoke Shoes	Mass Produced
Materials	Hardwoods, cast iron	Hardwoods	High-density polyethylene, aluminium, fiberglass

SHOE OVERVIEW

SHOE PARTS

Parts		Function	Common Materials
	Shoe lace	The most common fastening component of a shoe.	Leather, woven fabric, polypropylene ropes, webbing
	Upper	The upper helps hold the shoe onto the foot. It is connected to the sole by a strip of leather, rubber, or plastic that is stitched between it and the sole, known as a welt.	Calf, hide, kid (leather shoes), heavyweight woven fabrics such as cotton, linen, canvas, cotton drill (fabric shoes), polypag, neoprene, Lycra, Spandex (sports shoes & sneakers)
	Lining	The lining covers the inside seams of a shoe, but linings made of special materials also tout comfort features such as additional padding, or the ability to pull moisture away from the foot.	Sheepskin, pigskin, fabric
	Toe Puff & Heel Stiffener	The puff and the stiffener provide support and help to retain the shape of the shoe.	Thermoplastic materials, fierboard board with adhesive coating
	Insole	The insole is attached to the lasting margin of the upper, which is wrapped around the last during the closing of the shoe during the lasting operation.	Leather, fiberboard
	Shank	Together with the insole, the shank is the foundation of a shoe. It helps to strengthen the shoe between the back and the joint.	Wood (low heel), fiberboard (low heel), fluted steel (high heel)
	Midsole (Optional)	Provides cushioning and shock absorption.	Ethylvinyl Acetate (EVA)
	Outsole / Sole Unit	The outsole is the layer in direct contact with the ground. It may comprise of a single piece, or may be an assembly of separate pieces, often of different materials.	Leather, vegetable-tanned leather, rubber, rubber cupsoles (sport shoes), thermoplastic resin (TPR) and polyurethane (PU), brown polyurethane, wood, cork, PVC
	Heel	The heel provides support for the heel of the foot.	Wood, nylon or polycarbonate with steel central core, metal, cork, Perspex

PUMP ANATOMY

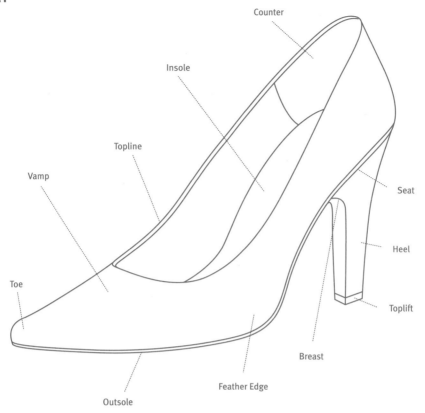

Counter

Insole

Topline

Vamp

Seat

Heel

Toplift

Toe

Breast

Outsole

Feather Edge

EXPLODED VIEW OF A PUMP

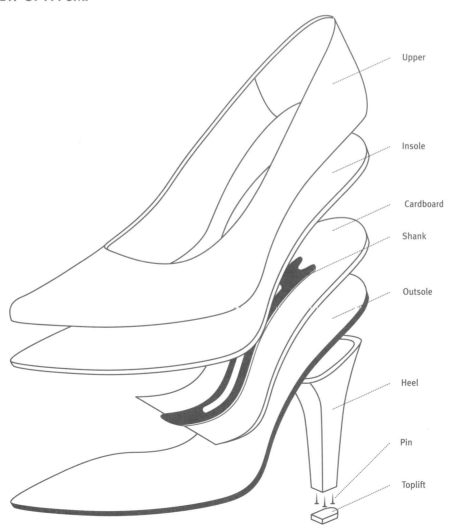

Upper

Insole

Cardboard

Shank

Outsole

Heel

Pin

Toplift

DERBY SHOE ANATOMY

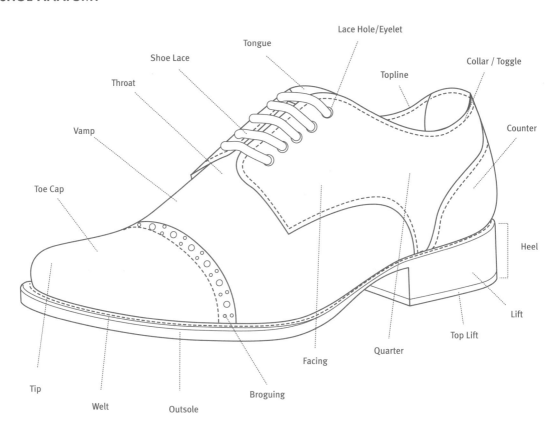

Lace Hole/Eyelet

Tongue

Shoe Lace

Throat

Topline

Collar / Toggle

Vamp

Counter

Toe Cap

Heel

Lift

Top Lift

Facing

Quarter

Tip

Broguing

Welt

Outsole

EXPLODED VIEW OF A DERBY SHOE

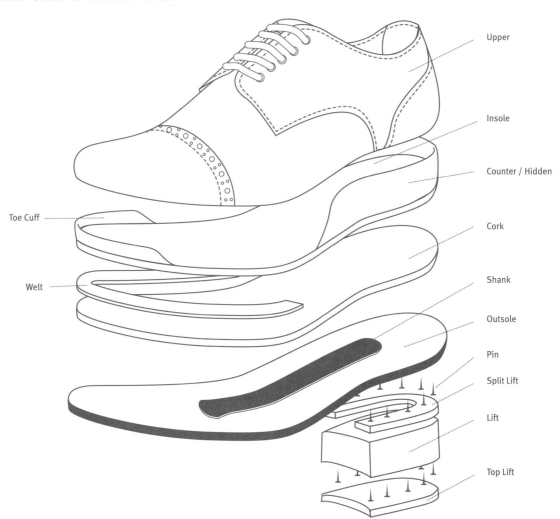

Upper

Insole

Counter / Hidden

Toe Cuff

Cork

Shank

Welt

Outsole

Pin

Split Lift

Lift

Top Lift

TRAINER ANATOMY

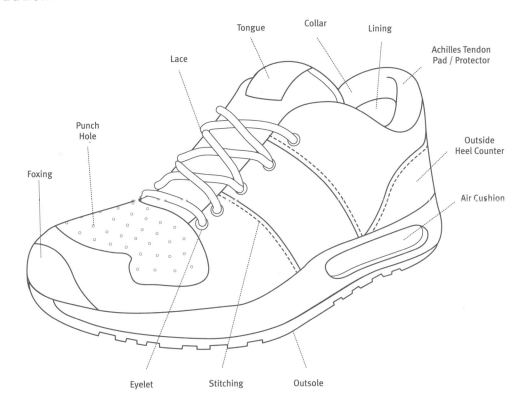

Tongue
Collar
Lining
Achilles Tendon
Pad / Protector

Lace

Outside
Heel Counter

Punch
Hole

Air Cushion

Foxing

Eyelet   Stitching   Outsole

EXPLODED VIEW OF A TRAINER

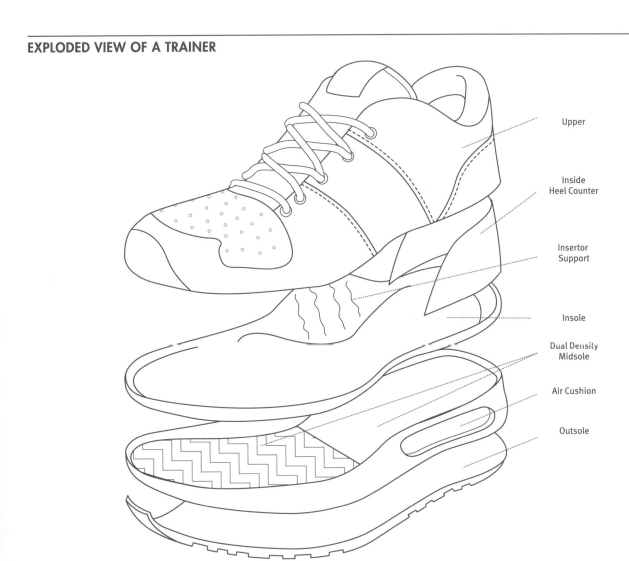

Upper

Inside
Heel Counter

Insertor
Support

Insole

Dual Density
Midsole

Air Cushion

Outsole

SHOE MANUFACTURING

SHOE MANUFACTURING PROCESS

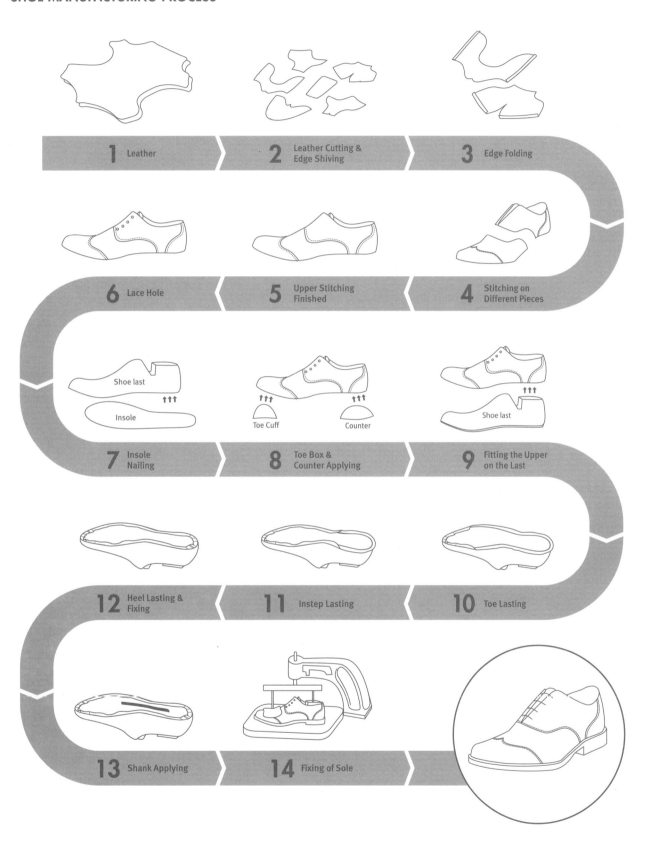

1 Leather

2 Leather Cutting & Edge Shiving

3 Edge Folding

6 Lace Hole

5 Upper Stitching Finished

4 Stitching on Different Pieces

Shoe last
Insole

Toe Cuff
Counter

Shoe last

7 Insole Nailing

8 Toe Box & Counter Applying

9 Fitting the Upper on the Last

12 Heel Lasting & Fixing

11 Instep Lasting

10 Toe Lasting

13 Shank Applying

14 Fixing of Sole

Shoemaking videos on Fashionary Youtube Channel:
http://youtube.com/user/Fashionaryonline/playlists

SHOEMAKING TOOLS

GLUE

Brush

Used for brushing rubber adhesive on leather.

Plastic Spreader

Used for spreading rubber adhesive on leather.

Rolling Spreader

For applying uniform pressure to the surface of adhesive.

Adhesive

A rubber solution that is used in upper preparation and a stronger synthetic rubber adhesive is used for sole attaching.

All Purpose Cement

Designed originally for attaching soles, the cement is easy to spread, non-smearing, extremely flexible and versatile.

FASTENING

Waxed Linen Thread

A durable waxed linen thread which works smoothly through leather.

Tack

Used for securing the upper to the insole in the initial stages of lasting.

Hand-Stitching Needle

It has an extra large needle hole which is suitable for thicker threads, e.g. waxed thread.

Glovers' Needle

Used for piercing and passing through tough materials such as leather, suede and vinyl without tearing.

Curved Needle

Used for lacing on leather, especially along sharp edges.

PUNCHING & MARKING

Stitching Chisels

Features steel blades for punching lacing slits.

Compass

A measuring tool that can be opened to any required width and used to create a parallel line as a guide for cutting.

Overstitcher

It moves along leather to mark the spacing of stitches for smooth, even results.

Multi-Hole Punch

A punch for punching holes of different sizes on leather.

Adjustable Groover

Used for spacing hand stitching holes and running over completed stitches to give them a machine-sewn look. The groove width is adjustable.

Adjustable Creaser

For creating parallel lines and inside borders.

Masking Tape

An adhesive tape with a slight stretch.

Oval Punch

Punches for punching holes of different sizes on leather.

Silver Marking Pen

A pen with silver ink used to mark guidelines on upper pieces.

Awl

A pointed tool used for piercing patterns or materials to create location points as a guide for cutting or stitching.

BURNISHING

CMC

Burnishing Gum in powder form.

Burnishing Gum

It is applied on leather surfaces or edges for glossy and smooth finish.

MISCELLANEOUS

Bone Folder

A tool made from plastic or bone used to assist the turning over and pleating of a folded edge.

Sharpening Stone

A stone rod used to sharpen the edge.

Cleaning Brush

A brush used to clean any dust or dirt.

EDGING

Common Edge Tool

Bevels and rounds off edges of straps and all soft leather.

French Edge Tool

Makes beveled edges at any desired angles including mitre-joints.

Emery Board

A board used for polishing and smoothing edges.

NT Dresser

Contains a sanding plate for polishing and smoothing edges.

Leather Edge Paint

Gives a pleasing finish to the edges of leather goods.

CUTTING & LASTING

Tack Knife

A knife for removing lasting tacks.

Trimming Knife

Used for removing any irregularities under the shoe after lasting.

Clicking Knife

A curved blade cutting knife designed for cutting leather.

Scalpel

A cutting knife with a very sharp blade, used for pattern cutting.

All Purpose Leather Knife

A knife used as a skiver. Round beveled, hand sharpened edges.

Round Knife

With a very sharp blade, the round knife is used for cutting leather and pattern.

Skiving Knife

A tool for skiving.

Square Point Knife

A square point blade designed for cutting leather.

Seam Ripper

It is equipped with both a steel hook & pointed blade for cutting or ripping.

Curved Lip Shoe Knife

A tool with a bent tip to trim shoe soles and uppers with ease.

Curved Scissors

A pair of scissors used for trimming the lining of the upper and cutting thread.

Leather Scissors

A pair of super sharp blades for cutting lighter weight leather.

Self Healing Cutting Mat

A self-healing synthetic cutting surface used for pattern cutting.

Poly Cutting Board

Used as a base to punch into when using stitching chisels.

Lasting Pincer

The lasting pincer grips the upper and pulls it over the insole in the lasting process.

MEASURING & MARKING

Steel Ruler

A ruler strong enough to retain a perfect straight edge for cutting.

Measuring Tape

A flexible tape made from a non-stretch material.

HAMMERING

French Pattern Hammer

A hammer that flattens any creases that appear during the lasting process.

Wood Mallet

Used for punching lacing slits on leather.

Folding Hammer

A handheld round-ended hammer used to flatten a folded edge.

SHOE CONSTRUCTIONS

BLAKE CONSTRUCTION

Pros: More flexible & lightweight. Easy to construct. Cheap.
Cons: Non water-resistant. Not suitable to be done by hand.
Example: Loafer
Details: The outsole is directly stitched to the insole. A single stitch attaches everything together.

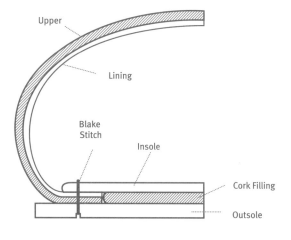

BLAKE / RAPID CONSTRUCTION

Pros: Flexible & lightweight. More durable. Easy to resole.
Cons: Non water-resistant. Less flexible.
Example: Loafer, Slip-on, Derby, Oxford
Details: The outsole is directly stitched to the insole. A single stitch attaches everything together.

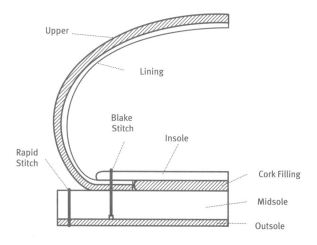

GOODYEAR WELT CONSTRUCTION

Pros: Fine construction. Easy to resole. Strong. Slightly waterproof.
Cons: Much longer production time than cheaper alternatives.
Example: Loafer, Slip-on, Derby, Oxford
Details: The construction uses stitching to hold the upper leather, lining leather and welt to the ribbing that is bonded to the insole. The welt is then stitched to the leather or rubber sole.

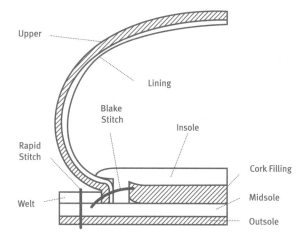

NORWEGIAN / STORM CONSTRUCTION

Pros: Waterproof. Sturdy.
Cons: Complex construction. Time consuming.
Example: Country boots, Hiking boots
Details: By turning the upper inside out and laying a welt on top, a seal is created to improve water resistance. It is employed by a small number of Italian shoemakers for its aesthetic.

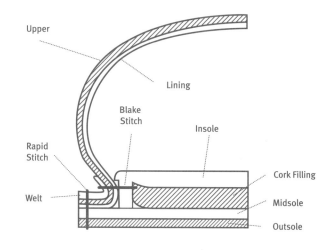

STITCH DOWN CONSTRUCTION

Pros: Waterproof. Sturdy. Touch.
Cons: Complex construction. Time consuming.
Example: English Country Boot, English Hiking Boot
Details: Similar to the Norwegian construction, instead of laying the welt on top of the upper, the welt is stitched underneath the upper.

BOLOGNA CONSTRUCTION

Pros: Very flexible. Lightweight. Cheap.
Cons: Not waterproof. Not durable.
Example: Moccasins, Slippers
Details: The leather upper is wrapped around the bottom and sewn up. Then the sole is sewn directly to the upper. Similar to Blake construction except the stitching is closer to the edge on the inside of the shoe.

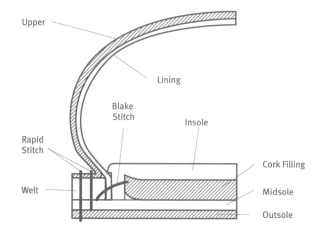

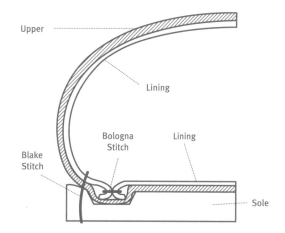

TYPES OF STITCHING ALONG TOPLINE

Single Needle Topstitching

Double Needle Topstitching

Zig Zag Lockstitch

Binding Edges & Single Needle Topstitching

EDGE FINISHING & SEAM TREATMENTS

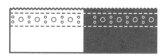

Gimped edge with two or one punch
(also described as brogueing)

Folded edge with single punch row

Piped edge with a single punch

Raw edge piping

Raw edge piping with ponyskin

Edge bound with ponyskin

Raw edge with contrasting raw edge leather trim

Edge Bounding

Lap Seam

Closed Seam

Run & Turned seam (blind seam)

Seam piped with ponyskin

SHOE PATTERNS

PATTERN OF A FLAT PUMP

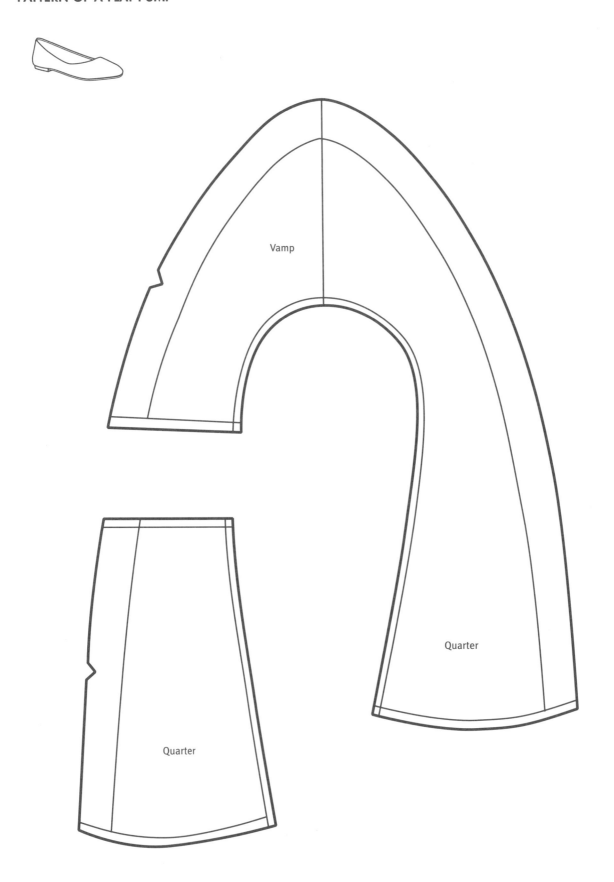

Vamp

Quarter

Quarter

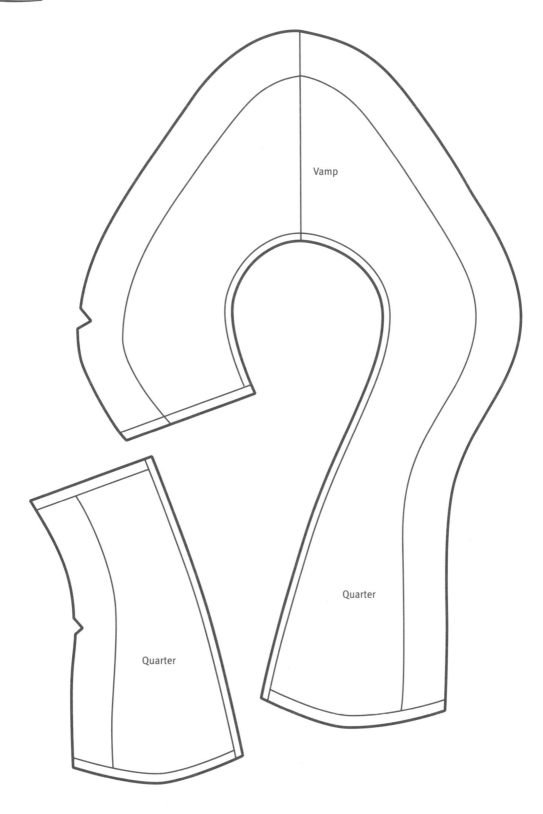

Vamp

Quarter

Quarter

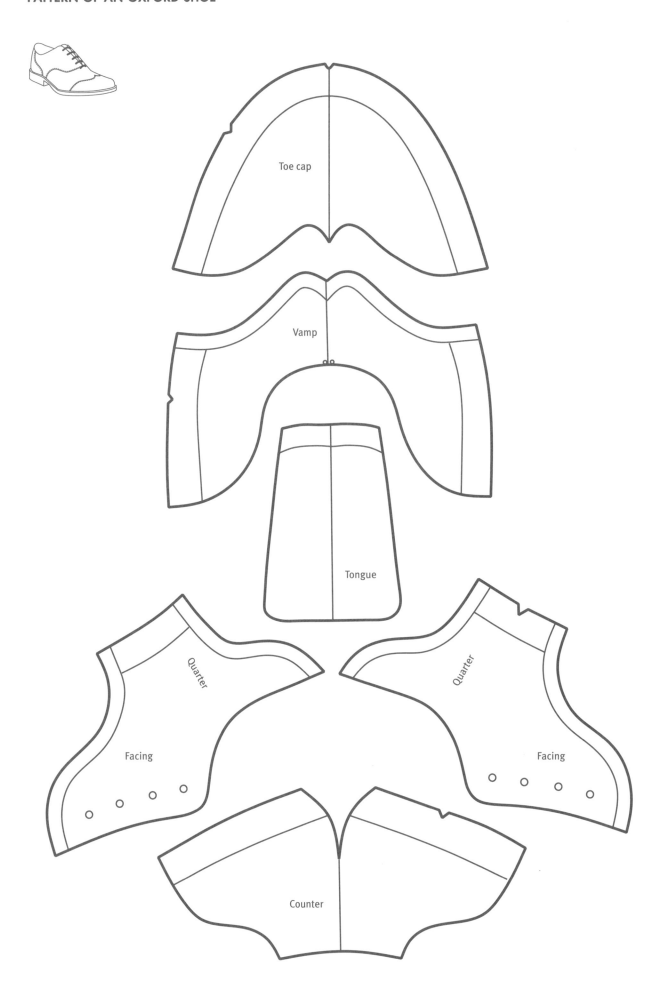

Toe cap

Vamp

Tongue

Quarter

Quarter

Facing

Facing

Counter

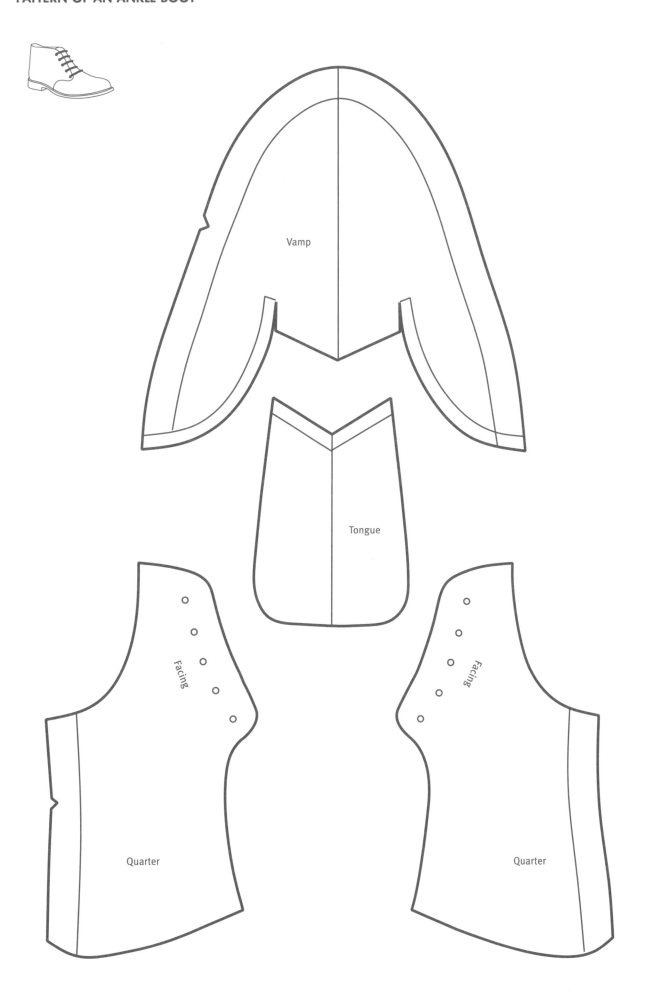

Vamp

Tongue

Facing

Facing

Quarter

Quarter

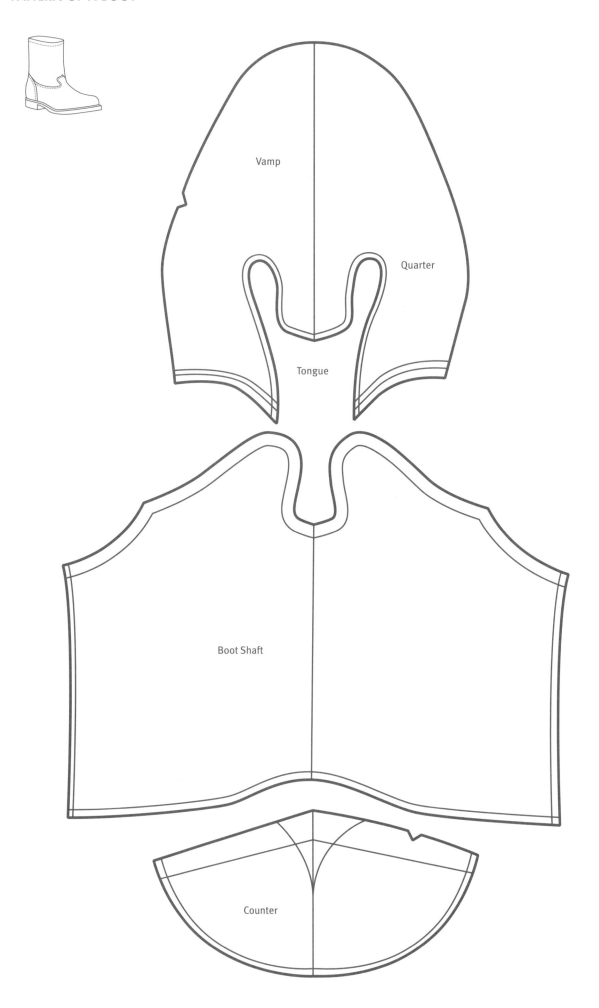

Vamp

Quarter

Tongue

Boot Shaft

Counter

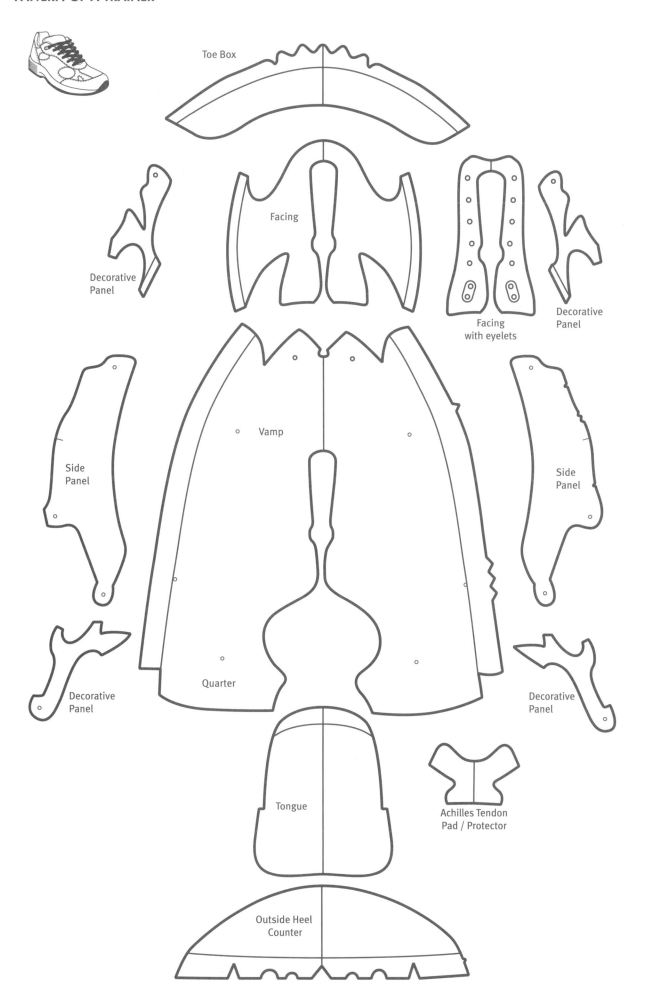

Toe Box

Facing

Decorative
Panel

Facing
with eyelets

Decorative
Panel

Vamp

Side
Panel

Side
Panel

Decorative
Panel

Quarter

Decorative
Panel

Tongue

Achilles Tendon
Pad / Protector

Outside Heel
Counter

LEATHER OVERVIEW

SUBDIVISIONS OF LEATHER

A - Butt ············· Best Value, 13% of the hide
B - Bend ············ Good Value, 30% of the hide
C - Shoulder ········ Fair Value, 32% of the hide
D - Head, Belly ····· Poor Value, 25% of the hide
——→ ················· Grain line

COMMON TANNING METHODS

Vegetable-tanned leather

Vegetable-tanned leather is tanned using tannins and other ingredients found in different vegetable matter, such as tree bark prepared in bark mills, wood, leaves, fruits and roots and other similar sources.

Chrome-tanned leather

Also known as wet blue, Chrome-tanned is the most common tanning method due to its cost and time needed. It is more supple and pliable than vegetable-tanned leather and does not discolor or lose shape as drastically in water as vegetable-tanned leather. More esoteric colors can be dyed.

Aldehyde-tanned leather

Also known as wet white, Aldehyde-tanned leather is tanned using glutaraldehyde or oxazolidine compounds. The leather is often seen in automobiles and shoes for infants.

Rawhide

Rawhide is made by soaking thin skin into lime and then stretching it while it's dry. It is stiffer and more brittle than other forms of leather. It can be cut into cord and produced as shoelace.

CLASSIFICATION OF LEATHER

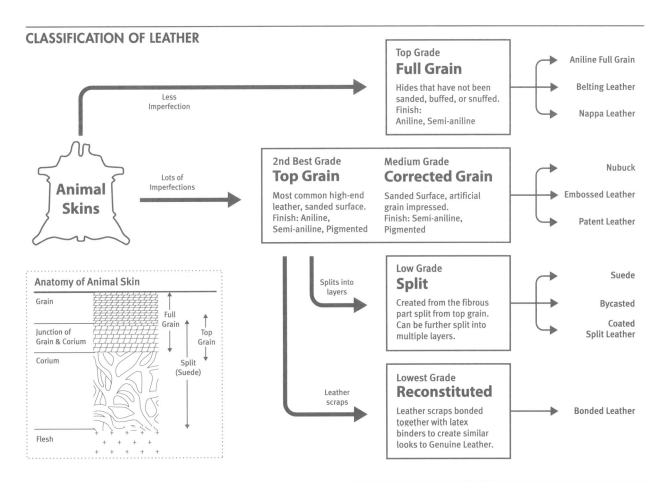

Animal Skins

Less Imperfection →

Top Grade — Full Grain
Hides that have not been sanded, buffed, or snuffed.
Finish: Aniline, Semi-aniline
→ Aniline Full Grain
→ Belting Leather
→ Nappa Leather

Lots of Imperfections →

2nd Best Grade — Top Grain
Most common high-end leather, sanded surface.
Finish: Aniline, Semi-aniline, Pigmented

Medium Grade — Corrected Grain
Sanded Surface, artificial grain impressed.
Finish: Semi-aniline, Pigmented
→ Nubuck
→ Embossed Leather
→ Patent Leather

Splits into layers →

Low Grade — Split
Created from the fibrous part split from top grain. Can be further split into multiple layers.
→ Suede
→ Bycasted
→ Coated Split Leather

Leather scraps →

Lowest Grade — Reconstituted
Leather scraps bonded together with latex binders to create similar looks to Genuine Leather.
→ Bonded Leather

Anatomy of Animal Skin

Grain
Junction of Grain & Corium
Corium
Flesh

Full Grain
Top Grain
Split (Suede)

GRADING SYSTEM

A Grade - No imperfection / marks or scars
B Grade - 5-10% imperfection
C Grade - 10-20% imperfection
D Grade - 20-30% imperfection
E Grade - 30-40% imperfection
F Grade - Factory rejected

THICKNESS SYSTEM CONVERSION

Ounces	Thickness	Ounces	Thickness	Ounces	Thickness
1	0.4 mm	6	2.4 mm	11	4.4 mm
2	0.8 mm	7	2.8 mm	12	4.8 mm
3	1.2 mm	8	3.2 mm	13	5.2 mm
4	1.6 mm	9	3.6 mm	14	5.6 mm
5	2.0 mm	10	4.0 mm	15	6.0 mm

LEATHER TYPES

CATTLE

Most leather is made of cattle skin, structure varies across the whole hide, strong.

Usage: Shoe upper, shoe sole & lining

CALF

Slightly rubbery, fine grain, little variation across the skin.

Usage: Higher quality men's, women's dress shoes & insole

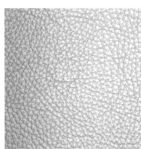

BUFFALO

Strong, tough, rubbery feel, pebbly appearance, thick.

Usage: Shoe upper, especially for boots

GOAT

Strong, thin, fine grain, regular pattern, papery feel.

Usage: Shoe upper. Vegetable tanned goat skin is used for linings.

SHEEP

Good heat insulation. Thin, soft, loose fibrous structure. Loose grain surface and light substance with soft feel, very porous. Low durability.

Usage: Shoe upper, lining

LAMBSKIN

The softest, thinnest, most supple type of skin. Buttery texture and finely grained. Elastic, very form-fitting, stretches well and tends to reshape after wearing.

Usage: Shoe upper

DEERSKIN

Tough, soft, supple, very stretchy. Washable and abrasion resistant.

Usage: Boots, indoor shoes

ELK

Similar to deerskin except very heavy and much thicker.

Usage: Indoor shoes

PIGSKIN

High breathability. Soft, thin, supple, durable, relatively tough with tight grain. Common hide for suede.

Usage: Quality footwear, lining

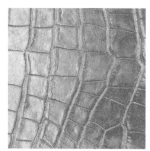

ALLIGATOR

Thick in the bend and thin in the belly and limbs. Scaly, supple (belly), tough, durable.

Usage: Luxury shoes upper

SNAKE

Great variation according to the type of snake, distinctive pattern, lightweight, strong, papery feel.

Usage: Luxury shoes upper, decoration

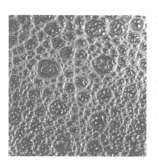

FROG / TOAD

Lightweight, thin, strong, great variation according to the type of species.

Usage: Luxury shoes upper, decoration

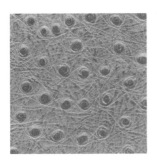

OSTRICH

One of the finest and most durable types of skins in the world. Unique bumpy texture. Flexible, pliable, durable and soft, very strong.

Usage: Shoe upper

KANGAROO

Very strong (10 times the tensile strength of cowhide and is 50% stronger than goatskin), thin, lightweight, uniform fiber structure.

Usage: High performance soccer footwear, UGG

SALMON

Fine scales, pliable, strong and elegant looking. The most popular fish leather.

Usage: Shoe upper

PERCH

Sourced from Nile. Thick, large & soft round scales.

Usage: Shoe upper

WOLFFISH

Smooth skin, scaleless. Easily recognizable thanks to its dark spots and 'stripes' which are due to the friction of marine rocks.

Usage: Shoe upper

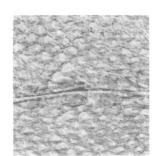

COD

Its skin has finer scales than salmon, but its texture is more varied, sometimes smooth and sometimes rough.

Usage: Shoe upper

EEL

Very smooth in touch with an elegant horizontal pinstripe-like pattern. Lightweight, supple, incredibly strong. Sewn together to create a leather panel.

Usage: Luxury shoes upper

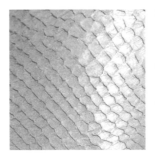

TILAPIA

Compared with salmon skin, the pattern of tilapia leather is more beautiful, but the skins are smaller in size.

Usage: Luxury shoes upper

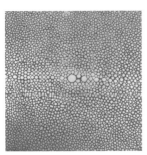

STINGRAY

Distinctive pattern. Highly durable (25 times more durable than cowhide leathers) and has a unique supple texture.

Usage: Luxury shoes upper

RABBIT

Small in size, thin and fragile.

Usage: Lining, decoration

LIZARD

Strong, lightweight, papery feel & thin.

Usage: Luxury shoes upper, decoration

HORSE

Tough, thin, non-uniform quality, stretches well, Commonly used for making shoes.

Usage: Luxury shoe upper

SHOE LACES & EMBELLISHMENTS

LACING METHODS

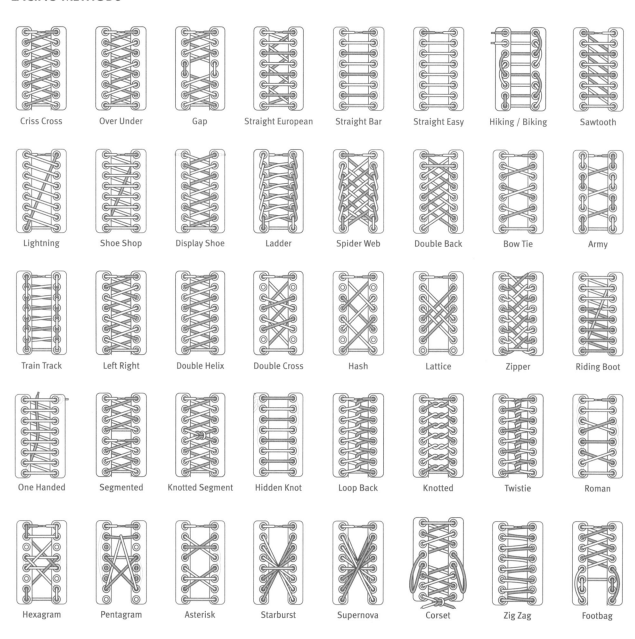

Criss Cross	Over Under	Gap	Straight European	Straight Bar	Straight Easy	Hiking / Biking	Sawtooth
Lightning	Shoe Shop	Display Shoe	Ladder	Spider Web	Double Back	Bow Tie	Army
Train Track	Left Right	Double Helix	Double Cross	Hash	Lattice	Zipper	Riding Boot
One Handed	Segmented	Knotted Segment	Hidden Knot	Loop Back	Knotted	Twistie	Roman
Hexagram	Pentagram	Asterisk	Starburst	Supernova	Corset	Zig Zag	Footbag

LACE LENGTH RECOMMENDATION

	Narrow 25mm (1 inche)	Medium 50mm (2 inches)	Wide 75mm (3 inches)
2 pairs of eyelets	60 cm (24")	70 cm (28")	80 cm (32")
3 pairs of eyelets	60 cm (24")	80 cm (32")	100 cm (39")
4 pairs of eyelets	70 cm (28")	90 cm (35")	110 cm (43")
5 pairs of eyelets	80 cm (32")	100 cm (39")	130 cm (51")
6 pairs of eyelets	80 cm (32")	110 cm (43")	140 cm (55")
7 pairs of eyelets	90 cm (35")	120 cm (47")	160 cm (63")
8 pairs of eyelets	90 cm (35")	130 cm (51")	170 cm (67")

** Information by Ian's Shoelace Site - http://fieggen.com/shoelace

SIZES

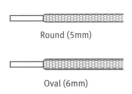
Round (5mm)

Oval (6mm)

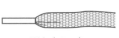
Flat (8mm)

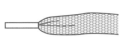
Wide (12mm)

Extra Wide (15mm)

SHOE LACE ACCESSORIES

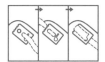

Lace Anchor

Shoelace Charm

Safe Lace

Zero-friction Fitting

Snap-n-step

Tyless Locking Button

Tassel Shoelaces

Tie Buddies

TYPES OF SHOE LACE

| Waxed | Velvet | Organza | Leather | Bubble | Caterpy Run Bubble Active | Telephone Line | U-Lace · Elastic Segments | Lock Laces | Hickies |

BUCKLES

| Buckle Set | Fashion Buckle | Half Roller Buckle | Double Tongue Roller Buckle | Full Skate Buckle | Half Solid Brass Buckle | Full Shoe Buckle | Full Buckle | Brass Slide | Full Slide |

RINGS

| Flat Ring | Light Ring | Heavy Ring | Solid Brass Ring | Split Ring |

D-RINGS

| Heavy Dee | Light Dee | Solid Brass Dee | Unwelded Dee | Welded Dee |

KEEPERS

| Wire Keeper | Wide Wire Keeper |

EYELETS & WASHERS

| Small Eyelet & Washer | Large Eyelet & Washer | Oval Eyelet & Washer | Floral-Shaped Eyelet& Washer | Ski Loop |

PRESS STUDS

Button Stud Socket Eyelet

Baby Durable Dot Snap Fasteners

Press Button

RIVETS

| Bifurcated Rivet | Pyramid Rivet | Double Capped Rivet | Tubular / Self Piercing Rivet |

SHOE CARE

SHOE CARE & ACCESSORIES

Wax Shoe Polish

Protects and nourishes leather to produce a long-lasting glossy shine.

Cream Shoe Polish

Protects and nourishes leather to produce a long-lasting glossy shine similar to that of satin.

Saddle Soap

The soap is used for cleaning, conditioning and softening leather, particularly that of saddles and other horse tack.

pH Bal. Leather Cleaner

Matches the pH of your leather to better preserve the leather's strength, durability and appearance.

Leather Conditioner

Lubricates and protects all top coated/protected leather. Makes leather look and feel like new.

All Purpose Shoe Cleaner & Conditioner

Cleans and preserves grained, gloved, patent, and smooth leathers while preventing salt stains and water spotting.

Suede Cleaner

Effectively removes dust and dirt from all types of suede & nubuck leathers.

Suede Protector

Provides maximum protection against water and stains, for suede and nubuck.

Leather Dye

Restores color and finish to worn leather before polishing.

Leather Preparer and Deglazer

An all-purpose cleaner and stripper for leather articles. Can be used to de-glaze factory finishes from shoes, purses, holsters, saddles, etc.

Season Leather Protector

Protects, conditions and waterproofs all full-grain leather footwear. Natural beeswax allows leather to breathe; will not weaken or decay any boot materials.

Reptile Leather Cleaner

Used for cleaning exotic leathers such as alligator, snake, lizard, ostrich, eel, etc.

Patent Leather Cleaner

Used for cleaning patent leather.

Shoe Shine Sponge

Gives an instant shine to leather, vinyl shoes and accessories including bags, luggage, and briefcases of any color.

Horsehair Shine Brush

Used for buffing the shine out of shoes.

Horse Hair Circular Dauber Brush

The brush can spread shoe polish evenly and thoroughly.

Shine Cloth

The cloth brings up a brilliant shine after polishing and spit shining.

Foam Polish Applicator

Used for applying paste or cream shoe polish quickly and easily.

Shoe Stretcher

A tool for making a shoe longer or wider or for reducing discomfort in areas of a shoe.

Shoe Tree

Placed inside the shoe when it is not being worn, the shoe tree helps maintain the shoe's shape.

Heel Grip

The grip prevents the shoe from slipping on the heel if the fit is not perfect.

Shoe Insert

Insert of various materials for cushioning, improved fit, or reduced abrasion. Inserts may also be used to correct foot problems.

Overshoes

A rubber covering placed over shoes for rain and snow protection.

Shoe Bag

A bag that protects shoes against damage when they are not being worn.

Shoehorn

Helps insert a foot into a shoe by keeping the shoe open and providing a smooth surface for the foot to slide upon.

SHOE MAINTENANCE

HOW TO USE A SHINE CLOTH

Remove dirt on the shoe
Use 3 fingers to hold the shine cloth and rub on the shoe.

Apply shoe polish on the shoe
Fold the shine cloth into quarters. Use 3 fingers to hold the shine cloth and rub on the shoe for polishing.

Apply shoe conditioner
Use 2 fingers to hold the shine cloth and rub on the shoe gently.

Bring up shine after polishing
Fold the shine cloth into its thickest. Hold the cloth in your fist and rub on the shoe gently.

POLISHING SHOES

Tools required

Shoe Tree ....
Shine Cloth ....
Horsehair Shine Brush ....
Shoes Wax Polish ....
Leather Conditioner ....

1
Put a shoe tree into the shoe. Remove any dirt/mud/salt with a brush or damp rag. Wait until dry.

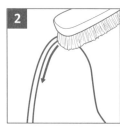

2
Remember to remove the dirt along the edges of the sole and shoe's edges.

3
Rub a moist cloth in the polish to acquire a small amount on the cloth.

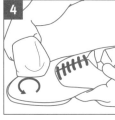

4
Apply the polish in small circles, in small amounts.

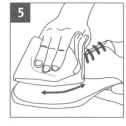

5
Fold the cloth into quarters and gently rub around the shoe.

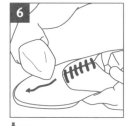

6
Apply the shoe conditioner and rub it gently.

7
Use the brush to rub around the shoe to make sure the shoe conditioner is absorbed thoroughly.

8
Fold the shine cloth into its thickest. Hold the cloth in your fist and rub on the shoe gently to give shine to the shoe.

9

FINISHED

IF THE COLOR ALONG SOLE EDGES ARE FADING

Tools required:

Shine Cloth ···············
Shoes Wax Polish ···········
Leather Dye ··············

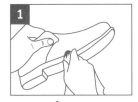

1

2

Remove dirt along the edges of the sole. Apply leather dye along the edges.

Use a shine cloth to rub along the edges.

IF WRINKLES APPEAR AFTER WEARING

Tools required:

Shoe Tree ··············
Shoe Soap ··············
Shoe Shine Sponge ········

1

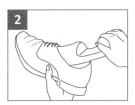

2

Wet the sponge and rub it along the wrinkles. Use a shoe soap to wash away the dust and then clean it.

Put a shoe tree into the shoe when it is still wet. Adjust the shape of the shoe and leave it to dry overnight.

IF SHOES BECOME MOLDY

Tools required:

Towel ··················
1:1 Vinegar & Water ·······

1

2

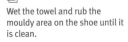

Wet the towel and rub the mouldy area on the shoe until it is clean.

Mix equal parts vinegar to equal parts water. Moisten a soft cloth with the mixture and use it to wipe the surface.

IF THE SHOE SOLE IS TOO SLIPPERY

Tools required:

Fine Grained Sandpaper ···
Rubber Sole Guard ········
Shoe Adhesive ··········

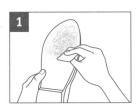

1

2

3

Rub the sole with a piece of fine grained sandpaper.

Apply shoe adhesive to the entire surface area of the half sole.

Immediately place the sole guard in position on the bottom of the shoe.

IF SHOES GET WATER MARKS AFTER RAINING

Tools required:

Sponge ················
Shoe Soap ··············
Shoe Tree ··············

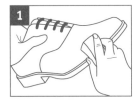

1

2

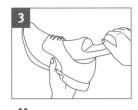

3

Dampen a sponge and rub around the entire shoe.

Use a shoe soap to rub around the shoe. Use a dry sponge to clean the bubbles.

Put the shoe tree into the shoe when it is still wet and leave to dry overnight.

PART VI

MISCELLANEOUS

SHOE LABELS

PARTS OF FOOTWEAR

Upper

Lining & Sock

Outer Sole

MATERIAL USED

Leather

Coated Leather

Textile

Other Material

LABEL EXAMPLES

SHOE BOX LABEL EXAMPLES

BOOKS & BOOKMARKS

BOOKS

Dictionary
- The Complete Footwear Dictionary

Science & Technology
- The Science of Footwear
- A Manual of Shoemaking and Leather and Rubber Products
- Archaeological Footwear
- Boot Making and Mending
- Craft Manual of North American Indian Footwear
- Crafting Handmade Shoes
- Decorate Your Shoes: Create One-Of-A-Kind Footwear
- Footwear Design (Portfolio Skills: Fashion & Textiles)
- Handbook of Footwear Design and Manufacture
- Handmade Shoes for Men
- How to Make a Shoe (Classic Reprint)
- Pattern Cutter's Handbook
- Pattern Cutting: Step by Step Patterns for Footwear
- Shoe Making, Old and New
- Shoemaking
- The Altered Shoe Altered Shoe
- The Art of Boot and Shoemaking
- The Manufacture of Boots and Shoes
- The Mode in Footwear: A Historical Survey with 53 Plates

Collectible
- 100 Shoes
- Art of the Boot
- Catalogue of the footwear in the Coptic Museum
- Cowboy Boots: Art and Sole
- Cult Shoes: Classic and Contemporary Designs
- Custom Kicks: Personalized Footwear
- For the Love of Shoes
- High Heel Heaven
- High Heels: Fashion, Femininity & Seduction
- Kicks Japan: Japanese Sneaker Culture
- New Shoes: Contemporary Footwear Design
- Shoe Love: In Pop-Up
- Shoe Obsession
- Shoe Design
- Shoes: A Celebration of Pumps, Sandals, Slippers & More
- Shoes: A Lexicon of Style
- Sneaker Freaker: The Book 2002-2005
- Sneakers (Special Limited Edition)
- Sneakers: The Complete Collectors' Guide
- Stiletto
- The Complete Book of Shoes
- The Shoe Book

History
- A Foot in the Past
- Fashion Footwear: 1800-1970
- Feet and Footwear in Indian Culture
- Fifty Shoes that Changed the World
- Footwear
- Footwear Industry in Ireland, 1922-73
- Footwear, 1945-95: 50 Years History
- Footwear: Short History of European and American Shoes
- Frye: The Boots That Made History
- Heavenly Soles: Extraordinary 20th Century Shoes
- Heights of Fashion: A History of the Elevated Shoe
- History of Footwear in Norway, Sweden and Finland: Prehistory to 1950
- Made for Skate: The Illustrated History of Skateboard Footwear
- Shoe Innovations: A Visual Celebration of 60 Styles
- Shoegasm: An Explosion of Cutting Edge Shoe Design
- Shoes
- Shoes: A History from Sandals to Sneakers
- Shoes: A Visual Celebration of Sixty Iconic Styles
- Shoes: What Every Woman Should Know...
- Sneaker Book: Anatomy of an Industry and an Icon
- Sneakers
- Stepping Through Time: Archaeological Footwear from Prehistoric Times Until 1800
- The Seductive Shoe: Four Centuries of Fashion Footwear
- The Seductive Shoes: Four Centuries of Fashion Footwear
- The Sneaker Book: 50 Years of Sports Shoe Design
- Vintage Shoes: Collecting and Wearing Designer Classics
- Where'd You Get Those? New York City's Sneaker Culture: 1960-1987
- Women from the Ankle Down: The Story of Shoes and How They Define Us

Illustration
- Manolo Blahnik Drawings
- Shoe Fleur: A Footwear Fantasy
- Shoes, Shoes, Shoes
- Shoes: The Complete Sourcebook
- Shoestrology: Discover Your Birthday Shoe
- The Botanical Footwear of Dennis Kyte

Biography
- In My Shoes: A Memoir

Brands
- Adidas (Brands A to Z)
- Bally: Since 1851
- Beth Levine Shoes
- Blahnik by Boman: Shoes, Photographs, Conversation
- Brands A to Z - Trippen
- Christian Louboutin
- Jimmy Choo
- Manolo Blahnik
- Manolo's New Shoes
- Salvatore Ferragamo - Evolving Legend 1928-2008
- Shoe Designers
- Shoemaker of Dreams: the Autobiography of Salvatore Ferragamo
- Shoes A-Z: Designers, Brands, Manufacturers and Retailers
- Shoetopia: Contemporary Footwear
- Slam Kicks: Basketball Sneakers that Changed the Game
- The Sneaker Hall of Fame: All-Time Favorite Footwear Brands
- The Trainer Hall of Fame: All-Time Favourite Footwear Brands
- Vans: Off the Wall: Stories of Sole from Vans Originals
- Walking Dreams: Salvatore Ferragamo 1898-1960

Theory
- A Passion for Stilettos
- Bad Shoes & The Women Who Love Them
- Christian Lacroix and the Tale of Sleeping Beauty
- Do You Speak Shoe Lover: Style and Stories from Inside DSW
- European Union and Turkish Footwear Industry
- Feet and Footwear: A Cultural Encyclopedia
- How to start a Shoe Design Business
- Manolo Blahnik and the Tale of the Elves and the Shoemaker
- Sneaker Wars
- Things a Woman Should Know About Shoes
- Tutankhamun's Footwear: Studies of Ancient Egyptian Footwear

BOOKMARKS

Shoe Blogs
agirlsguidetoshoes.blogspot.com
barkingdogshoes.com
blog.aldoshoes.com
drshoereviews.com
essbeebeyourownlabel.com
heelcandy.com
leatherfoot.com/blog
mensluxuryshoes.com
myshoesblog.com
office.co.uk/blog
pursuitofshoes.com
r-a-wshoesblog.com
runningwithheels.com
seaofshoes.com
shoe-tease.com
shoeblogs.com
shoefanatic.co.uk
shoelust.us
shoeperwoman.com
shoesfromaroundtheglobe.com
shoesmitten.com
shoewawa.com

Shoe Blogs (cont'd)
talkshoes.com
theshoegirl.blogspot.com
theshoemaven.com
thesoulsofmyshoes.com
wgsn.com/blogs/footwear
wwd.com/footwear-news

Mens Shoe Blogs
aquila.com.au/freestyle
mensstylepro.com
oldleathershoe.com
mymanybags.blogspot.com

Shoes Reference
shoerazzi.com/see/blog

Shoelace
fieggen.com/shoelace

Fashion Blogs (Shoes related)
blogs.fidm.com/my_weblog/footwear_design
highsnobiety.com/category/footwear
blog.bergdorfgoodman.com/shoes

Shoe Info
shoeinfonet.com
virtualshoemuseum.com

Shoemaking
carreducker.blogspot.com
howtoshoes.blogspot.com
svetakletina.blogspot.com
redcoverstudios.com
shoemakingbook.com
theshoesnobblog.com
shoesandcraft.com
simpleshoemaking.com
simpleshoemaking.wordpress.com
stylisteph.wordpress.com
wikihow.com/Make-Shoes

TRADE FAIRS, MUSEUMS & COURSES

SHOE TRADE FAIRS

Country	City	Fair	Type	Month	Website
Australia	Melbourne/Sydney	Australian Shoe Fair	Footwear	Feb/Aug	australianshoefair.com
Canada	Toronto	Toronto Shoe Show	Footwear	Feb/Aug	www.torontoshoeshow.com
China	Dongguan	Dfm	Footwear	Apr	dfmshow.com
	Dongguan	China Shoes Dongguan	Footwear	Nov	chinashoesexpo.com
	Guangzhou	IFLE	Footwear	May	ifle-china.com
	Guangzhou	Shoes & Leather Guangzhou	Footwear	May	shoesleather-guangzhou.com
	Nigbo	Ningbo International Fashion Fair	Apparel	Oct	iffair.cn
	Shanghai	All China Leather Exhibition	Leather	Sept	aplf.com
	Shanghai	China International Footwear Fair	Footwear	Sept	aplf.com
	Shanghai	Fashion Accessories - Shanghai	Accessories	Dec	chinasourcingfair.com
	Shanghai	Intertextile Shanghai Apparel Fabrics	Apparel	Mar/Oct	interstoff.messefrankfurt.com
	Shanghai	Moda Shanghai	Accessories	Sept	aplf.com
	Shenzhen	Shenzhen International Apparel Fair	Apparel	Jul	szic.cn
France	Paris	Accessoires De Mode	Accessories	Apr	foiredeparis.fr
	Paris	Fatex	Fashion, Leather, Accessories	Jun	fatex.fr
	Paris	Mess Around	Shoes, Leather	Jan/Jun	theshow.whosnext.com
	Paris	Première Classe	Accessories	Mar/July/Oct	premiere-classe.com
Germany	Dusseldorf	GDS	Footwear	Mar/Sep	gds-online.com
	Dusseldorf	Global Shoes	Footwear	Mar/Sep	globalshoes-online.com
Hong Kong	Hong Kong	Fashion Accessories - Hong Kong	Accessoires	Apr/Oct	chinasourcingfair.com
India	Delhi	India International Leather Fair	Leather	Feb	iilfleatherfair.com
	Mumbai	India Shoes and Accessories Forum	Footwear, Accessories	Mar	www.isaf.in
Italy	Milan	Micam Shoe event	Footwear	Mar/Sep	www.micamonline.com
	Milan	Mipel	Leather	Mar/Sep	mipel.com
Japan	Tokyo	Fashion Goods & Accessories Expo	Accessories	Jul	fa-expo.jp/en
Russia	Moscow	Garderobe	Accessories	Apr/Oct	garderobe-expo.ru/en
	Moscow	Mosshoes	Footwear	Jan/Mar/Jun/Sep	mosshoes.com
Turkey	Istanbul	Aymod	Accessories, Footwear	Apr/Nov	cnraymod.com
	Istanbul	Aysaf	Accessories, Footwear	Feb/Sep	cnraysaf.com
	Istanbul	Bijoux Expo Turkey	Accessories	Sep	demosfuar.com.tr
UK	London	Pure London	Apparel, Footwear	Feb/Aug	www.purelondon.com
	Birmingham	Moda - Footwear	Apparel, Footwear	Feb/Aug	www.moda-uk.co.uk
US	New York	Accessorie Circuit	Accessories	Jan/Aug	www.enkshows.com/circuit
	New York	Accessories the Show NY	Accessories	Jan/Aug	accessoriestheshow.com
	Los Angeles	Transit / The LA Shoe Show	Footwear, Leather	Jan/Mar/Jun	www.californiamarketcenter.com/transit/
	New York / Las Vegas	Capsule	Footwear	Jan/Feb	capsuleshow.com
	New York / Las Vegas	Magic - Project Sole	Footwear	Jan	www.magiconline.com/project-sole-new-york
	New York	The Agenda Show	Apparel, Accessories	Jan	agendashow.com
	Atlanta	The Atlanta Shoe Market	Footwear	Feb/Aug	www.atlantashoemarket.com
Vietnam	Ho Chi Minh	IFLE - Vietnam	Footwear, Leather	Jul	ifle-vietnam.com
	Ho Chi Minh	Shoes & Leather Vietnam	Footwear, Leather	Jul	shoeleather-vietnam.com

SHOE MUSEUMS

Austria	Vienna Shoe Museum, Vienna
Belgium	SONS Museum (Shoes or No Shoes), Kruishoutem
Canada	Bata Museum, Toronto
Czech Republic	Zlín Shoe Museum, Zlín
France	Musee International de la Chaussure, Romans-sur-Isere
Finland	Vapriikki Shoe Museum, Tampere
Germany	German Shoe Museum, Hauenstein
Italy	Ferragamo Museum, Florence
Japan	Japan Footwear Museum, Fukuyama
Netherlands	International Wooden Shoe Museum, Eelde Virtual Shoe Museum, Zuid-Holland
Spain	Musei del Calzado, Alicante
Switzerland	Bally Shoe Museum, Schönenwerg
UK	Museum of London, London Northampton Museum & Art Gallery, Northampton Shoe Museum, Somerset The British Museum, London Victoria & Albert Museum, London
US	Brockton Shoe Museum, Brockton Costume Institute, New York

SHOE COURSES

Australia	Royal Melbourne Institute of Technology, Melbourne - Certificate in Custom made Footwear
France	Lycée de la Mode, Cholet - BTS Fashion Crafts - Footwear & Leather Goods
Italy	Istituto Europeo di Design - BA (Hons) Fashion Design (Major in Footwear Design)
	Polimoda, Florence - Undergraduate in Footwear and Accessories Design
	Cercal, San Mauro Pascoli - Professional Training Courses for Footwear and Leather Goods
Japan	Bunka Fashion College, Tokyo - Footwear Design Course
UK	London College of Fashion, London - BA (Hons) Cordwainers Footwear: Product Design and Innovation
	De Montfort University, Leicester - BA (Hons) Footwear Design
US	The Fashion Institute of Technology, NY - Bachelor of Fine Arts (BFA) degree in Accessories Design
	Fashion Institute of Design & Merchandising, California - Associate of Arts Advanced Study

SHOE SPEC SHEET

Date Sent	6th, August	Product Name	Platform Pump
Deadline	1st, October	Product Number	SS 1832 0001
Company	Fashionary Company	Sample Size	US Size 7
Season	Spring Summer	Last Model	Spring Line, #P412

A Side View

B Back View

C Front or ¾

Insole	#IN006	
Thread	Nylon 60 Red	
Finish 1		
Finish 2		

D Platform

80mm
32mm
30mm
28mm
60mm

E Heel

45mm
60mm
70mm
15mm
100mm

Description

	Material	Description
Upper	Red calf leather	Colour Code: RE001
Lining	Brown sheep skin	Colour Code: BR002
Zip		
Insole	Lamb nappa	Insole Code: IN006
Insole Binding		
Sock		
Heel	Pine Wood	Heel Code: HS032
Platform	Pine Wood	Platform Code: PA068
Sole		
Thread	Nylon 60 Red	

Notes

A	B	C
1. Folded edge	1. One piece counter 2. Top piece height : 5mm	1. Folded edge 2. Company logo print on it

D	E
The platform needed to be polished with matt finish wood wax	The heel needed to be polished with matt finish wood wax

Download the spec sheet - http://fashionary.org/downloads

RANGE PLAN

Company :	Fashionary Company				Season :	Spring Summer		
Product	Last Sample	Heel Shape & Design	Platform Shape & Design	Insole	Colourway	Price

Product	Last Sample	Heel Shape & Design	Platform Shape & Design	Insole	Colourway	Price
Product Number: SS 1833 0004 	**Last:** #P215 	**Heel:** #HB025 	**Platform:** #PA065 	Lamb nappa #IN006 	Colourway #1 Upper: Brown - BR003 Lining: Black - BK001 Colourway #2 Upper: Black - BK001 Lining: Red - RE002	US$258
Product Number: SS 1833 0005 	**Last:** #P426 	**Heel:** #HS032 	**Platform:** #PA068 	Lamb nappa #IN003 	Colourway #1 Upper: Pink - PK001 Lining: White - WT001 Colourway #2 Upper: Red - RE003 Lining: Black - BK003 Colourway #3 Upper: Blue - BU004 Lining: Black - BK003	US$180
Product Number: SS 1845 0001 	**Last:** #P426 	**Heel:** #HC022 		Lamb nappa #IN006 	Colourway #1 Upper: Black - BK003 Lining: Brown - BR001 Colourway #2 Upper: Red - RE006 Lining: Black - BK003	US$310

Download the range plan - http://fashionary.org/downloads

SHOE GLOSSARY

Aglet	A small plastic or metal sheath at the end of a shoelace, cord, or drawstring.
Aniline Leather	A type of leather which retains the natural signatures and skin structure of the original animal.
Ankle Boots	A type of boots which is ankle high while the shaft of the boot is absent.
Ankle Strap	A strap attached at the back of the shoe and goes around the ankle to provide heel retention.
Arch	A section of the foot between the ball and the heel that is curved to allow for the support of the body with the least amount of weight.
Athletic Shoes	A type of shoes designed for sports or other physical exercises.
Back Seam	A vertically stitched seam running down the center-back of shoes.
Ball	The padded section of foot between the arch and the toes.
Ballet Flats	It is derived from a woman's soft ballet slipper, with a very thin heel or the appearance of no heel at all.
Balmoral	A type of oxford shoes with a horizontal seam running across the quarters of the shoe.
Basketball Shoes	A type of athletic footwear designed for playing basketball. It comes in a variety of materials, designs, and even ankle heights, giving many options for different playing needs.
Bespoke Shoes	Shoes that are made on a shoe last that has been custom-made for an individual, rather than from the standard shoe last.
Blucher	A shoe with "open lacing" at the vamp. A Blucher and a Derby have a lot in common, but a Blucher does not have a gooseneck seam on the quarter.
Boat Shoes	Also known as deck shoes or topsiders, are typically canvas or leather with non-marking rubber soles designed for use on boats.
Bowling Shoes	The sole of the stationary foot is generally made of rubber to provide traction, while the sliding foot's sole is made of a smooth and flat material that allows the bowler to slide into the release with a rubber heel to allow for braking.
Break	A natural crease created on the leather upper of a shoe resulting from everyday wear.
Brogueing	Refers to the perforations or small punches that can be used to decorate a shoe.
Calluses	A hard area of skin that has been thickened by continual pressure, friction and use.
Cap Toe	Also known as a tip, a cap toe is a decorative piece of leather across the toe of a shoe.
Chelsea Boots	A type of close-fitting, ankle-high boots. There are elastic side panels and a tab of fabric at the back of the boot, enabling it to be slipped on and off.
Chukka Boots	A type of ankle-length boots with two or three pairs of eyelets for lacing. They are usually made from calfskin or suede.
Clogs	A type of footwear which is made in part or completely from wood traditionally. They usually have a big round toe and no fastening.
Collar	A piece of material stitched around the topline of the shoe. The collar can be padded to add extra comfort.
Contoured Footbed	An insole usually made of memory foam that molds to the shape of the foot for extra comfort and support.
Counter	A piece of material forming the back of a shoe to give support and stiffen the material around the heel.
Cowboy Boots	A specific style of riding boots, historically worn by cowboys. They have a Cuban heel, rounded to pointed toe, high shaft, and, traditionally, no lacing.
Crepe Sole	A type of sole typically made from rubber and made to resemble the texture of wrinkled crepe paper.
Croc Embossed	A leather decorative technique which gives it the impression of crocodile skin by stamping a pattern similar to crocodile skin onto the cow leather and then giving it a high-shine finish.
Cushioning	A shoe padding which is used to absorb foot strike forces and provides comfort and stability.
Derby Shoes	Also called Blucher in America, it is a type of shoe characterized by shoelace eyelet tabs that are sewn on top of a single-piece vamp. This construction method, also known as "open lacing",
Derby Shoes (cont'd)	contrasts with that of Oxfords.
Dress Boots	A short leather boot worn by men. It is built like dress shoes, but with uppers covering the ankle.
Dressing	Application of polish or gloss to a shoe to maintain its finish and appearance.
Duck Boots	Designed In 1912, Duck boots were created as a type of waterproof boot sold to hunters. The boots were made of lightweight waterproof leather uppers and rubber bottoms.
Elastic Gore	A flexible, elastic fabric that is sewn into the shoe's lining in order to provide a snug fit.
Espadrilles	A type of shoes in which the sole is made of jute rope. The jute rope sole is the defining characteristic of an espadrille.
Eyelet	A small hole through which aglets are threaded. They are often reinforced with a metal, plastic or rubber grommets.
Fiberboard	The material used for counters, insoles and heel lifts. It is primarily made of wood fibers.
Flat Foot	This is a medical condition where the arch of the foot has collapsed, leaving the entire foot to rest flat on the ground.
Folding Ballet Flats	Similar to ballet flats but with an elastic trim added along the topline.
Footbed	Also known as the insole, it refers to inside of the shoe where the foot rests.
Forefoot	The area in the front (fore) of the foot.
Foxing	A strip of rubber found on sneakers usually made from canvas. It joins the upper part of the shoe to the sole.
Full Grain Leather	A type of leather that has been tanned so that the natural texture, or grain, of the animal skin is visible.
Gait	Refers to a person's manner of walking.
Ghillie	It is originally worn by people in Ireland when they are dancing. They use laces which criss-cross the top of the foot and are tied together similar to a sneaker.
Gladiator Sandals	A type of T-strap sandals with several straps running across the front of the foot. These sandals were favored by Ancient Greeks and Romans.
Grain	The surface pattern on a piece of leather. Differs depending on the animal it came from.
Heel	The part of shoe that is attached under the heel of foot, and which varies in height and material according to the style of the shoe.
Heel-less	A type of high-heeled shoes, from which the heel is absent. Wearers have to put the weight on the toe instead of heel when walking.
Heel Breast	The side of the heel that faces forward when the shoe is on the foot.
Heel Counter	It is placed behind the heel of the foot, and is used to stiffen the back part of the shoe, and to maintain the shape of the shoe.
High-top Converse	Designed In 1917, the shoe was composed of a rubber sole and canvas upper and was designed to be an elite shoe for the professional basketball league.
Hiking Boots	Provides comfort for walking considerable distance over rough terrain, and protects the hiker's feet against water, mud, rocks, etc.
Huarache	It is a type of Mexican sandal. It has a woven-leather form on the upper.
Insole	The lining that adds comfort and arch support while separating the foot from the sole of the shoe.
Instep	The arched upper section of the foot found near the center between the toes and ankle.
Jelly	A translucent rubber-like plastic used in soles and as a filler in heels to add cushioning.
Jodhpur Boots	An ankle boot designed as a riding boot with a rounded toe and a low heel and fastened with a strap and buckle.
Kidd Leather	A type of leather made from the skin of young goats. It is very soft and mostly used for lightweight and casual footwear.
Kiltie Tassels Loafers	A type of slip on loafer which was first introduced as Aurlandskoen in Norway. It often features tassels on the front, or metal decorations.
Laces	A cord that is strung through eyelets in order to draw the shoe closed.
Last	A wooden or plastic block which represents the shape and size of

Last (cont'd)	the foot of the wearer. It is used during the process of shoemaking. It can be in standard sizes or bespoke.	**Shoe Horn** (cont'd)	easily.
Lasting Margin	The section of the upper which is tucked under and attached to the shoe's sole.	**Shoe Sizes**	An alphanumerical guidance indicating the fitting size of a foot.
Lining	The interior surface of a shoe.	**Shoe Tree**	A device used to resemble the shape of a foot. It is used to preserve the shape of the shoe and to stop it from developing creases by placing it into the shoe.
Loafers	Similar to the Moccasin shoe, which is a lace-less casual shoe.		
Loafer Pumps	A type a pump with the upper similar to loafers.		
Logger Boots	Also named Caulk Boots. It is a type of working leather nail-soled boots worn by loggers traditionally.	**Sipes**	A razor-cut pattern in outsoles of shoes, specifically deck shoes. These help to disperse water and prevent slipping.
Louis Heel	Developed in the seventeenth century, it is a heel fashioned from an extension of the shoe's sole.	**Slingback**	A strap that crosses behind the heel or ankle.
		Slip-ons	A type of shoes which are typically low and lace-less.
Low-top Converse	With the same features of the High-top version, the low-cut "oxford" version was designed in 1957 and is still manufactured today.	**Slippers**	A flat, casual shoe that slips on and is typically meant for use indoors.
		Slouch Boots	A type of shoe with a flexible boot shaft that rumples instead of standing upright.
Mary Jane	It is an American term for a closed, low-cut shoe with one or more straps across on the top.	**Sneakers**	A rubber-soled casual shoe made of soft, often man-made, materials, and used often for casual wear and sporting events.
Midsole	The layer of material located under the insole but over the outsole providing the shoe's main support and cushioning components.	**Soccer Shoes**	Also known as football boots. There are studs on the outsole of the shoes which could aid grip when running on grass.
Moc Toe	Structure similar to moccasins, but which lace-up instead of simply slipping-on.	**Sole**	The underside of the shoe. The term is also used to describe the bottom of the foot.
Moccasins	A casual shoe made from soft leather, with the sole brought up and attached to a piece of U-shaped leather on top of the foot, worn originally by American Indians.	**Spectators**	Made popular in the 1920's and 30's by Jazz and Swing musicians, they are a kind of shoe that is made from contrasting colored materials.
Mules	A type of shoe with a closed toe and no back, which allows the feet to just slide into them.	**Steel Toe**	A reinforced toe frequently found in industrial-style shoes designed to protect the foot and prevent injury in the workplace.
Nap Or Napped	A soft and fuzzy surface texture usually associated with leather or suede.	**Stilettos**	A stiletto heel is a long, thin, high heel found on some boots and shoes, usually for women.
Nubuck	A soft aniline dyed leather buffed to a suede-like condition. Easily susceptible to stains even after stain protection treatments.	**Suede**	A type of leather with napped surface, but may also indicate fabrics of a similar nap or brushed finish.
Opera Pumps	Also known as court shoes, it is a shoe with a low-cut front and usually without fastening.	**T-bar Pumps**	A closed, low-cut shoe with two or more straps forming a T shape.
Orthotic Insole	It is designed to straighten, improve, and support the foot.	**Tap**	A small partial sole which is normally made of metal or leather that is attached to the existing toe or heel of a shoe.
Outsole	The bottom of part of the shoe that touches the ground.		
Oxford Shoes	Also called "Balmoral" in America. It is characterized by shoelace eyelets tabs that are attached under the vamp, a feature termed "closed lacing". Oxfords are the standard shoe to wear with most suits.	**Tassel**	A knotted rope ornamental piece typically found on a shoe vamp.
		Thermoplastic - Rubber (T.P.R)	A type of plastic material used in injection molding processes. It is commonly used to sole safety shoes.
		Throat	Located at the central of the vamp which just proximal to the toe box. The throat of the shoe dictates the maximum girth permitted by the shoe.
Pecos Boots	The Pecos boots were introduced in 1953 and the boots were durable and practical, combining western style with the ruggedness of a work boot. There are ears on both sides of the boots.	**Tip**	Also known as a cap, a tip is another piece of material, usually leather, enclosing the toe of the shoe.
		Toe Box	The portion of the shoe that holds the toes.
Peep Toe	A type of shoe in which there is an opening at the toe-box.	**Tongue**	A strip of leather or other materials found under the laces of a shoe. The tongue is sew into the vamp and extends to the throat of the shoe.
Penny Loafers	A type of slip-on shoes, but the term penny loafer has uncertain beginnings. One explanation is that two pennies could be slipped into the slit, enough money to make an emergency phone call in the 1930's.		
		UGG Boots	It is known in Australia and New Zealand as a unisex style of sheepskin boots. They are typically made of twin-faced sheepskin with fleece on the inside, a tanned outer surface and a synthetic sole.
Perforations	Small holes punched into the shoe's leather, often on the toe, in order to add ornamental details to dress shoes.		
Pinking	The zig-zag finish found the edge or seams on the shoe.	**Upper**	All parts of a shoe above the sole that are stitched together.
Platform Shoes	A shoe, boot, or sandal with thick soles. They are often made of cork, plastic, rubber, or wood.	**Vamp**	It is the fore part of a shoe upper, normally a piece of leather that partially envelopes the foot.
Pumps	A type of shoes with a low-cut front and usually without fastening.	**Venetian Loafers**	It is a type of loafers without the ornamentation often found across the middle.
Quarter	The rear portion of a shoe comprising the part that covers the heel and is often joined at the back seam.	**Waist**	The part of the foot or shoe located between the ball and the instep, also known as the shank of the shoe.
Quarter Lining	A soft, inner lining of a shoe, typically made from leather or fabric.	**Wallabees**	Has been produced by Clarks shoes since 1967 and it comes in both shoe and boot versions. Both are made out of two pieces of leather or suede in the classic moccasin style, two eyelets and wedge sole.
Running Shoes	A type of shoes which is designed for running. There are different types of running shoes in the market, e.g. road running shoes and trail running shoes, while different features were added for improving the running experience.		
		Wedges	Shoes or boots with a sole in the form of a wedge so that one piece of material serves as both the sole and the heel.
Sandals	A type of footwear worn mostly in the warmer weather. It is in an open design that reveals most of the foot and toes and uses straps or strips or material to hold the shoe to the foot.	**Welt**	A strip of leather that is used to sew together the shoe's outsole and its insole and upper.
Scalloped, Scalloping	Similar to pinking, but a wavy cut instead of a zig-zag cut.	**Whole Cut Oxfords**	Instead of multiple pieces of leather being stitched together to make the upper, whole-cut oxfords are cut from just one piece for a hyper-clean look.
Shank	The supportive part of the shoe between the insole and outsole. It sits under the arch of the foot and gives the shoe structure.		
Sheepskin	A type of material made from the leather of sheephide used for making shoes and boots. Comes with or without the wool attached.	**Wing Tip**	A style of shoe with a toe that looks like a "W".
		Zero Drop	Refers to the thickness of the sole which the heel is less than a half inch in height. It allows the forefoot and heel to be the same distance from the ground.
Shoe Horn	A device used to allow a user to slip the foot into a shoe more		

SHOE LAST TEMPLATES

- ½" - 6" HEELS

- MEN'S POINTY TOE

- MEN'S SQUARE TOE

- MEN'S ROUND TOE

- MEN'S CHISEL TOE

- BOOT

- ATHLETIC SHOE

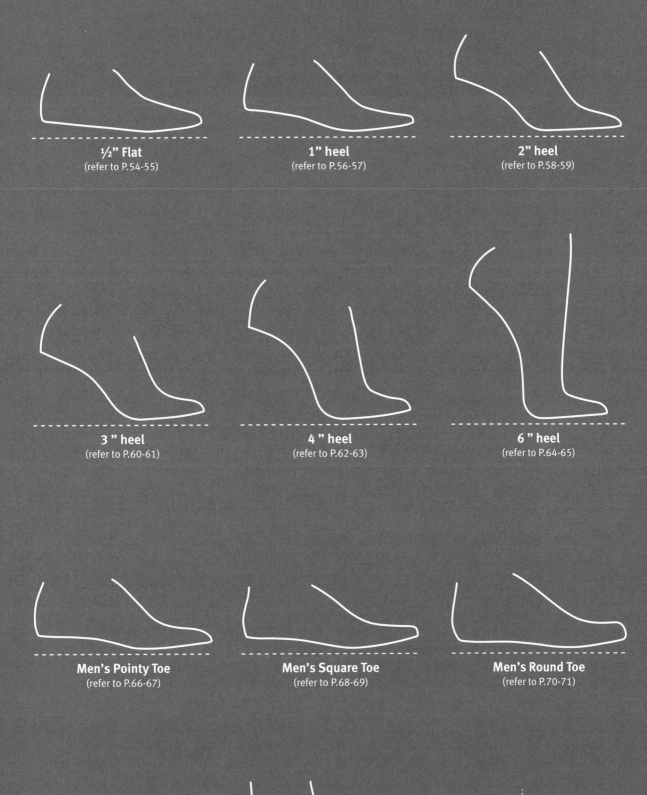

½" Flat
(refer to P.54-55)

1" heel
(refer to P.56-57)

2" heel
(refer to P.58-59)

3 " heel
(refer to P.60-61)

4 " heel
(refer to P.62-63)

6 " heel
(refer to P.64-65)

Men's Pointy Toe
(refer to P.66-67)

Men's Square Toe
(refer to P.68-69)

Men's Round Toe
(refer to P.70-71)

Men's Chisel Toe
(refer to P.72-73)

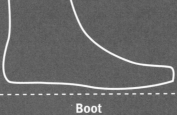

Boot
(refer to P.74-75)

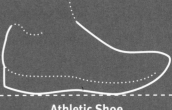

Athletic Shoe
(refer to P.76-77)

½" SHOE LAST TEMPLATES

Side View

Side View

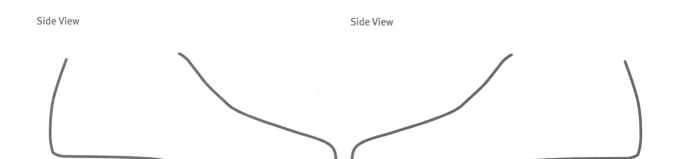

Side View

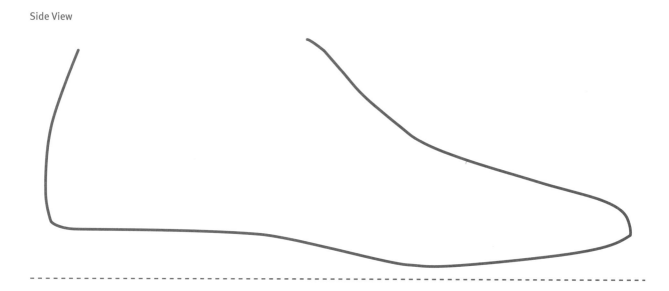

EXAMPLES

Top View

Back View

¾ View

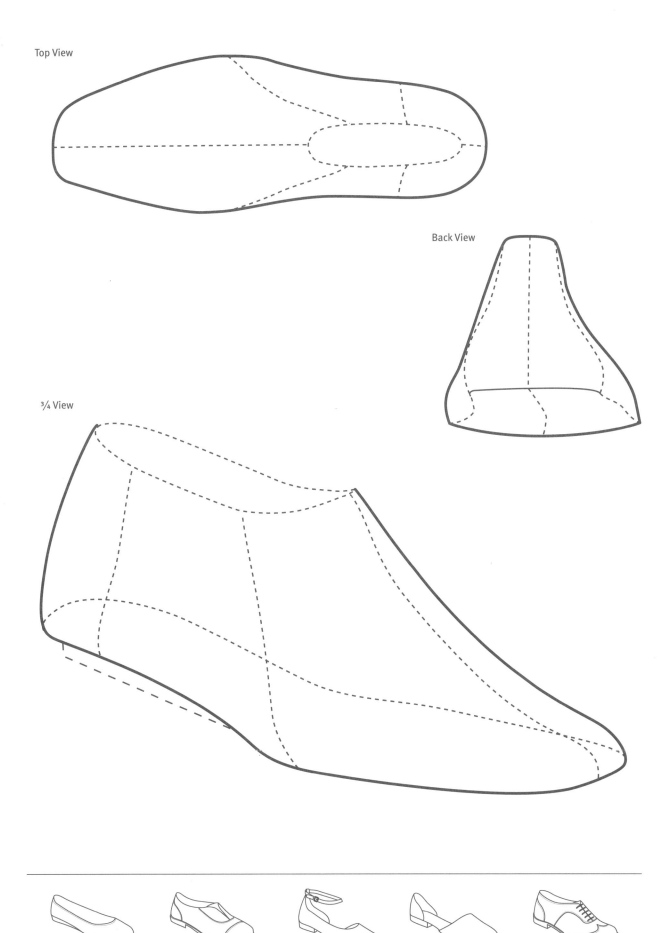

1" SHOE LAST TEMPLATES

Side View

Side View

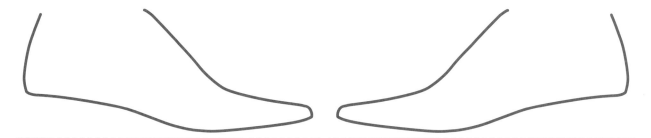

Side View

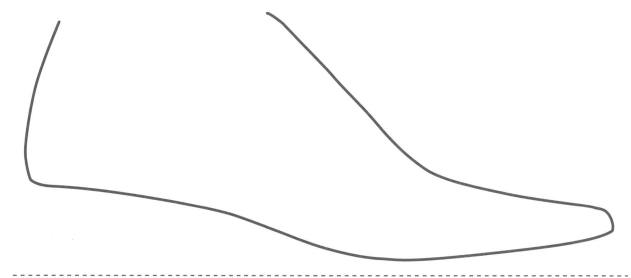

EXAMPLES

Top View

Back View

¾ View

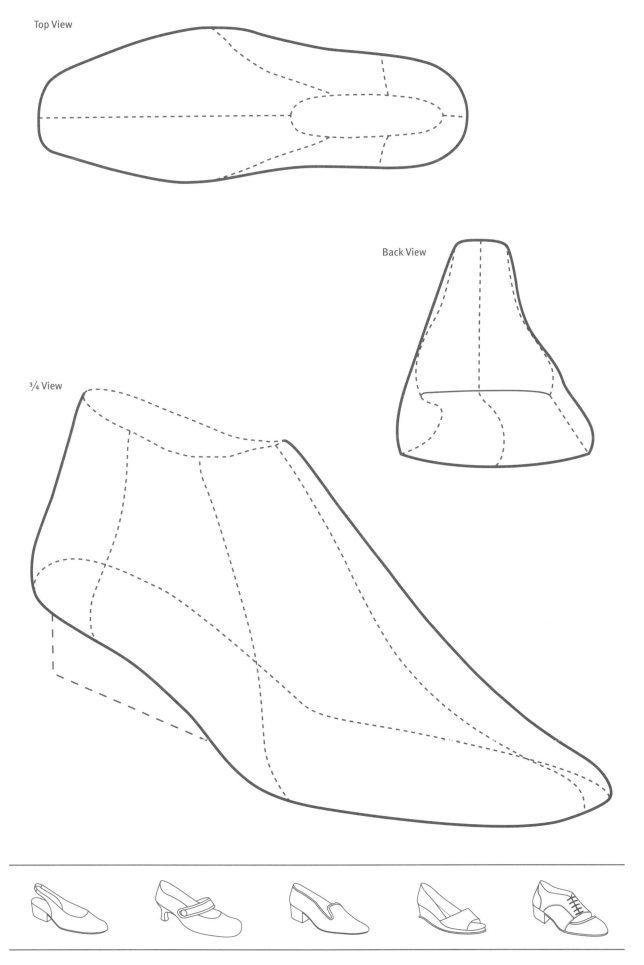

2" SHOE LAST TEMPLATES

Side View

Side View

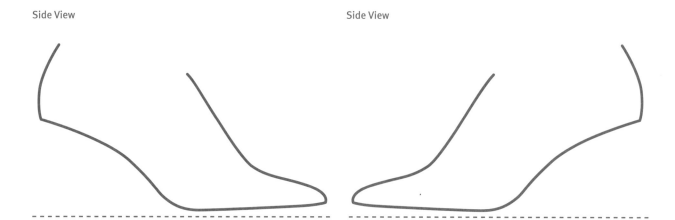

Side View

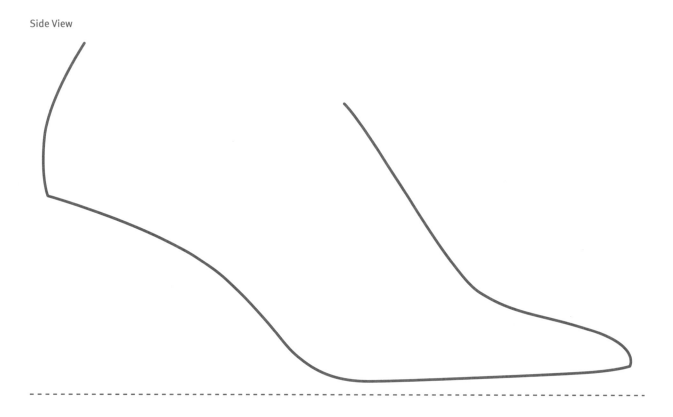

EXAMPLES

Top View

Back View

¾ View

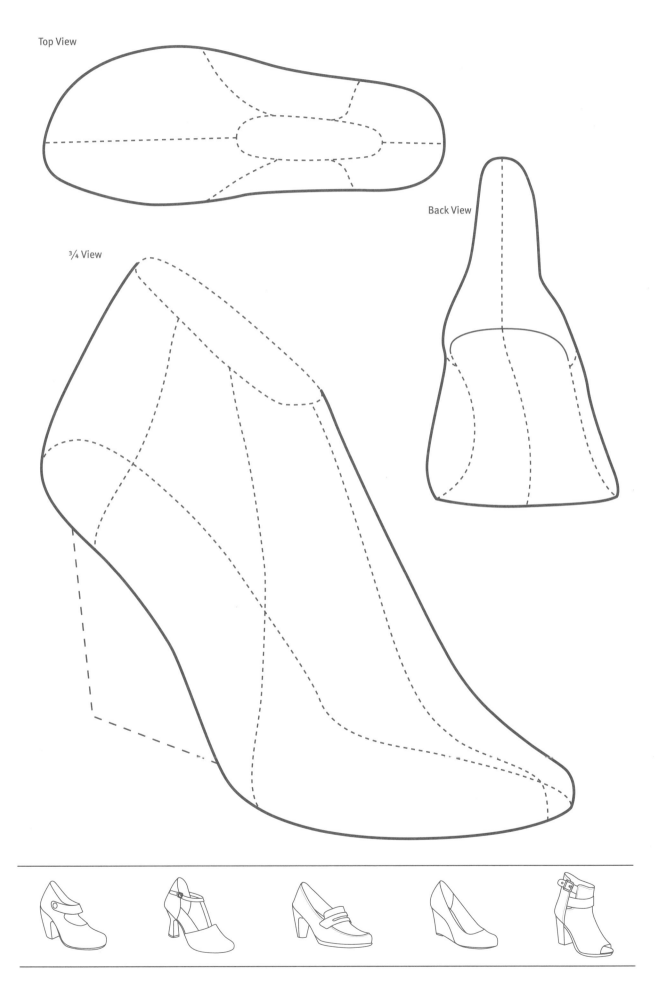

3" SHOE LAST TEMPLATES

Side View

Side View

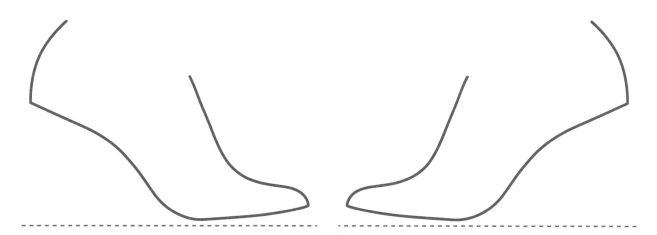

Side View

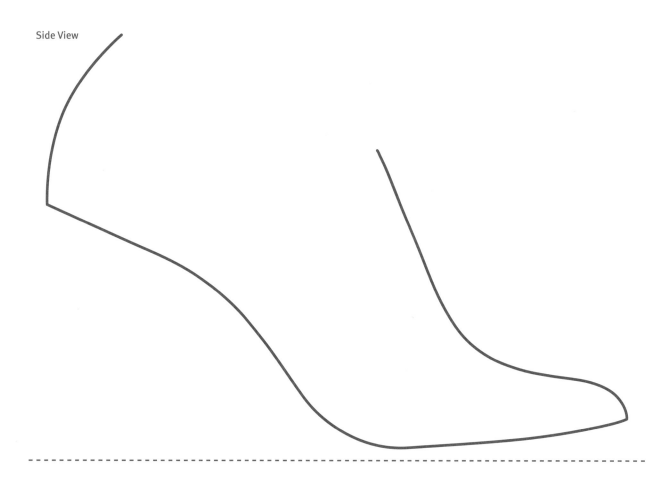

EXAMPLES

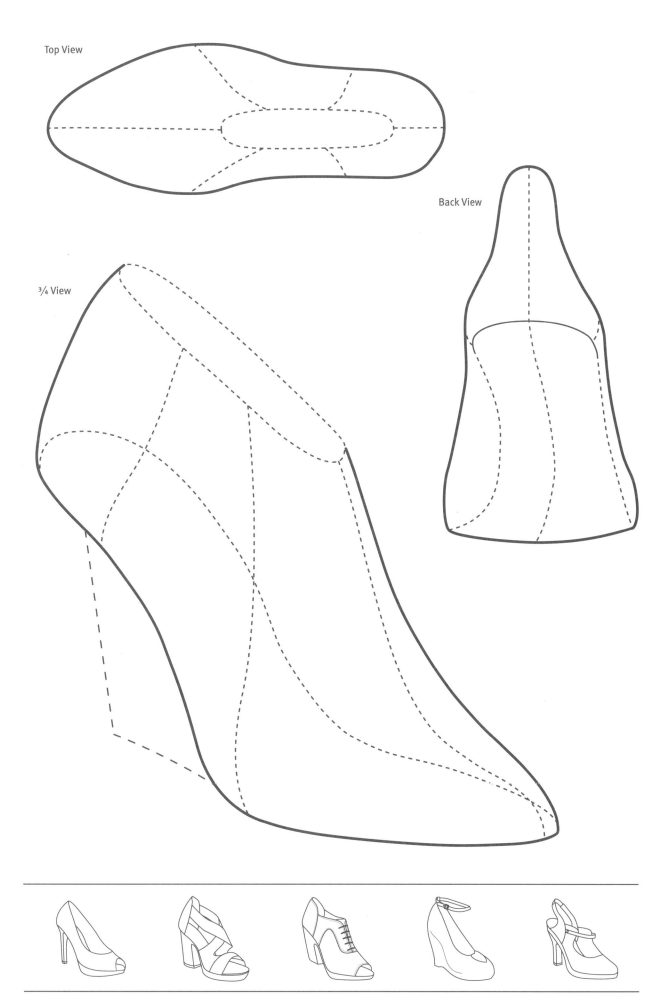

Top View

Back View

¾ View

4" SHOE LAST TEMPLATES

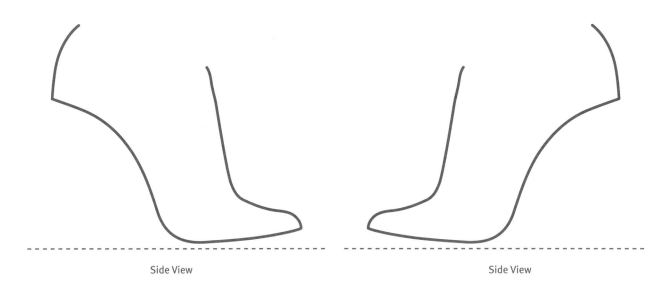

Side View

Side View

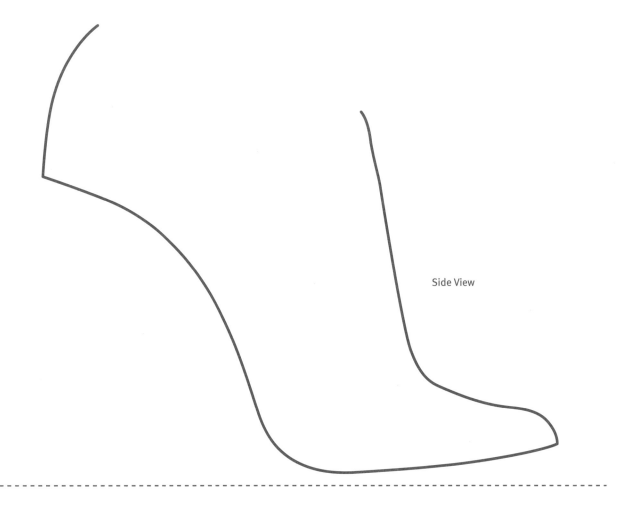

Side View

EXAMPLES

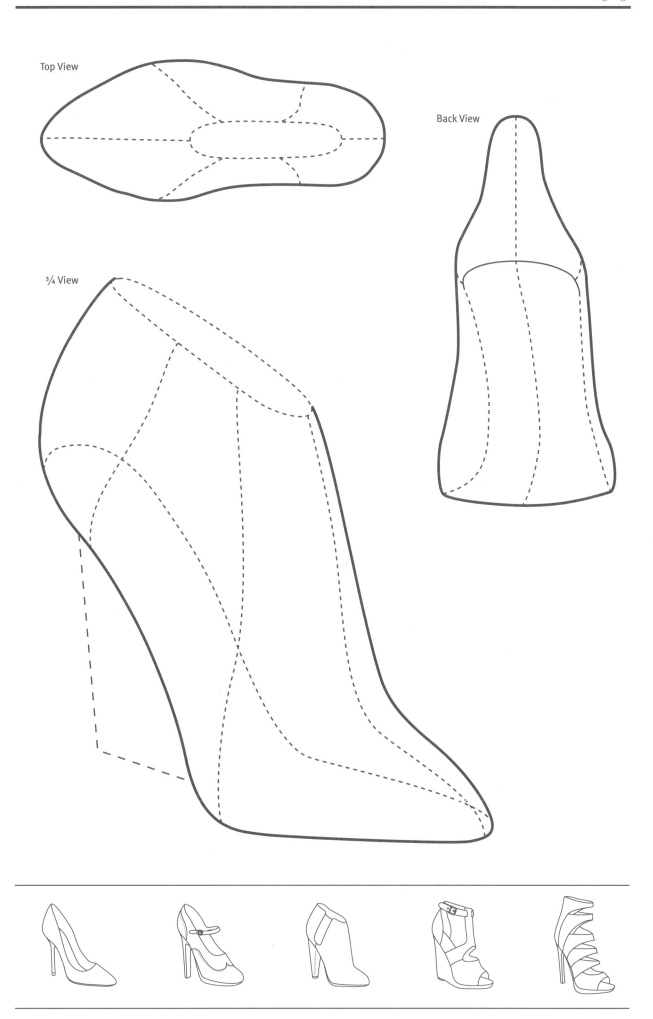

Top View

Back View

¾ View

6" SHOE LAST TEMPLATES

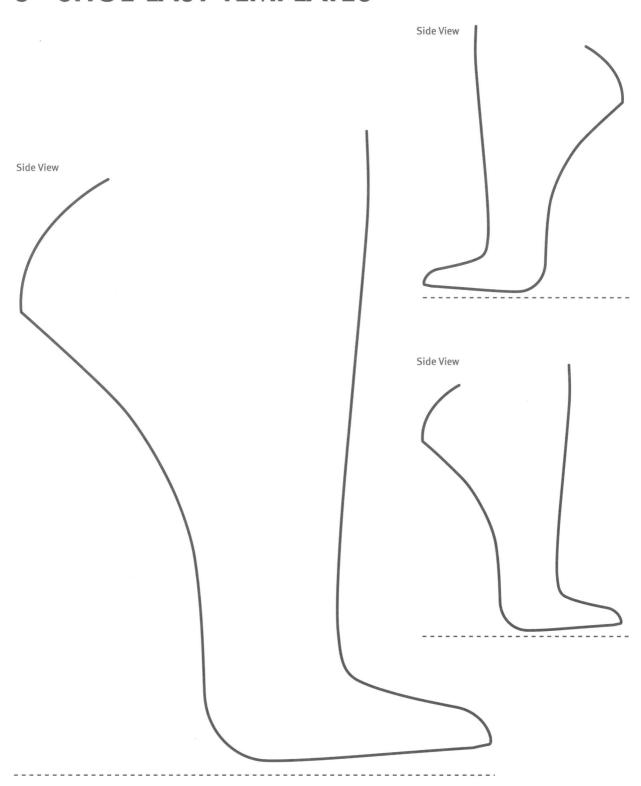

Side View

Side View

Side View

EXAMPLES

    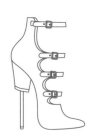

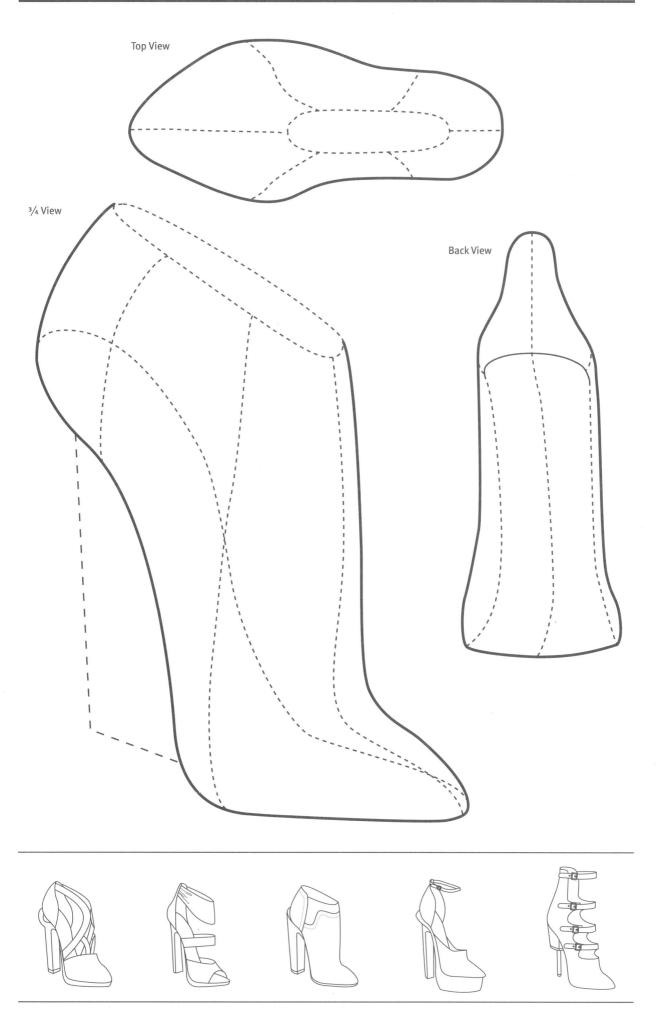

Top View

¾ View

Back View

MEN'S POINTY TOE LAST TEMPLATES

Side View

Side View

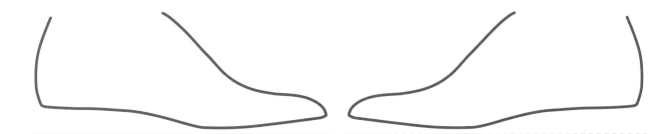

Side View

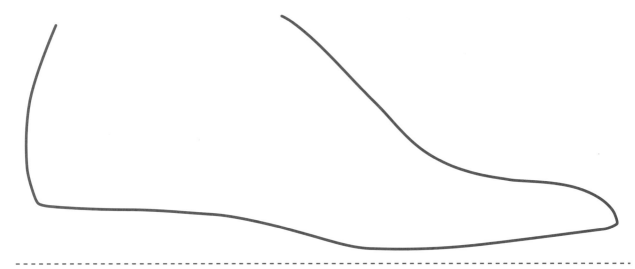

EXAMPLES

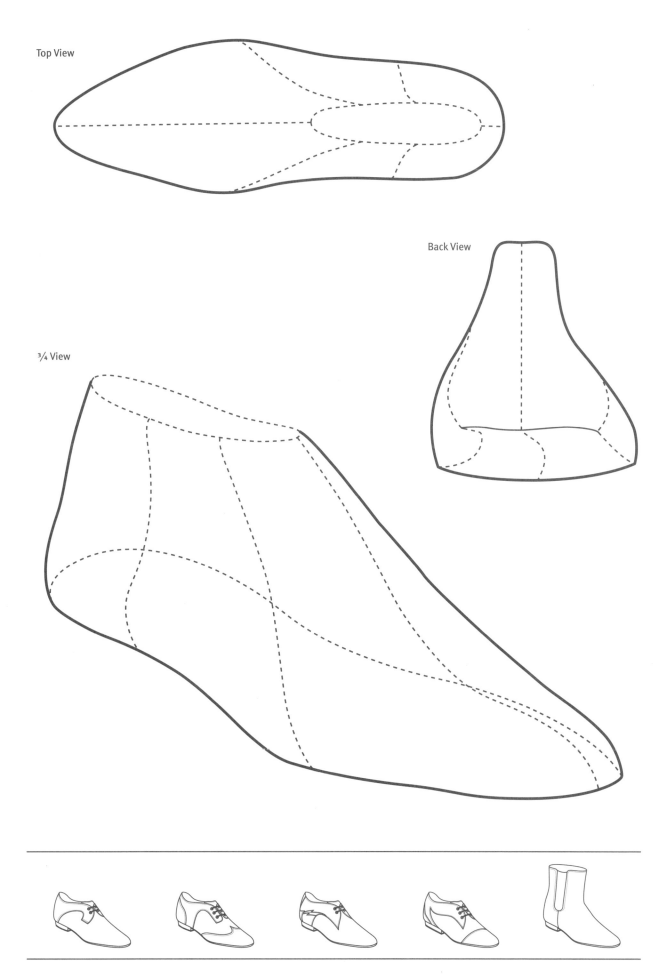

Top View

Back View

¾ View

MEN'S SQUARE TOE LAST TEMPLATES

Side View

Side View

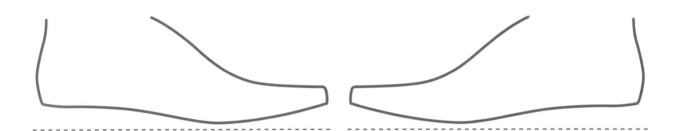

Side View

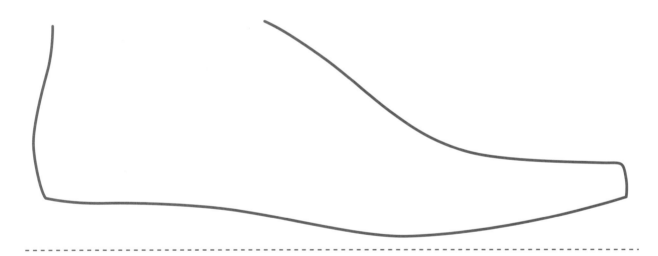

EXAMPLES

Top View

Back View

¾ View

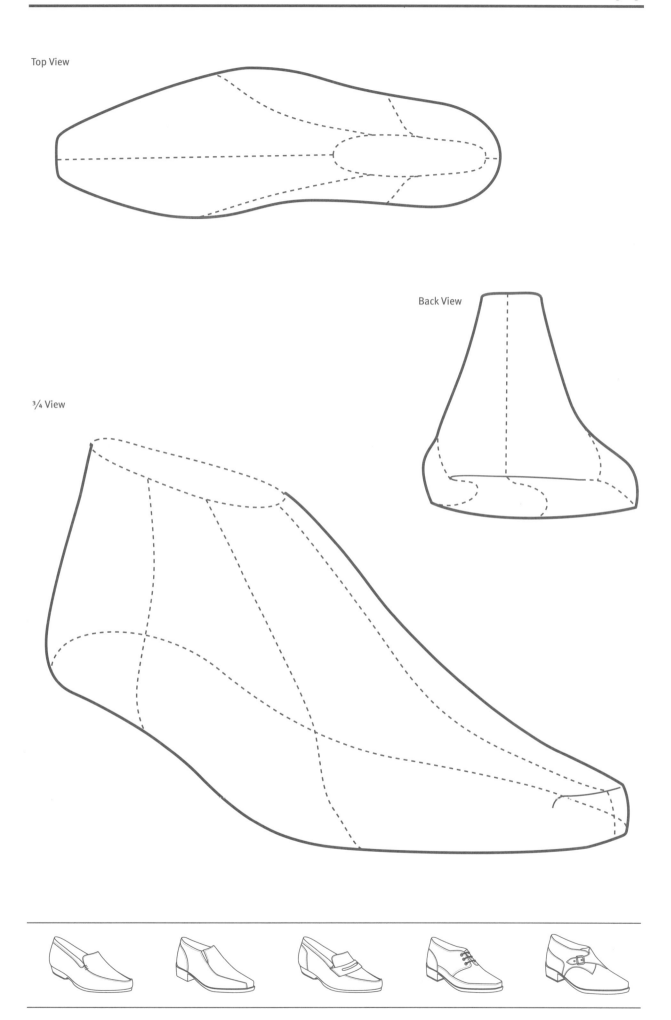

MEN'S ROUND TOE LAST TEMPLATES

Side View

Side View

Side View

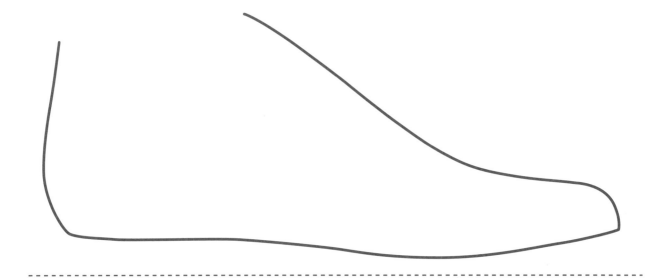

EXAMPLES

Top View

Back View

³/₄ View

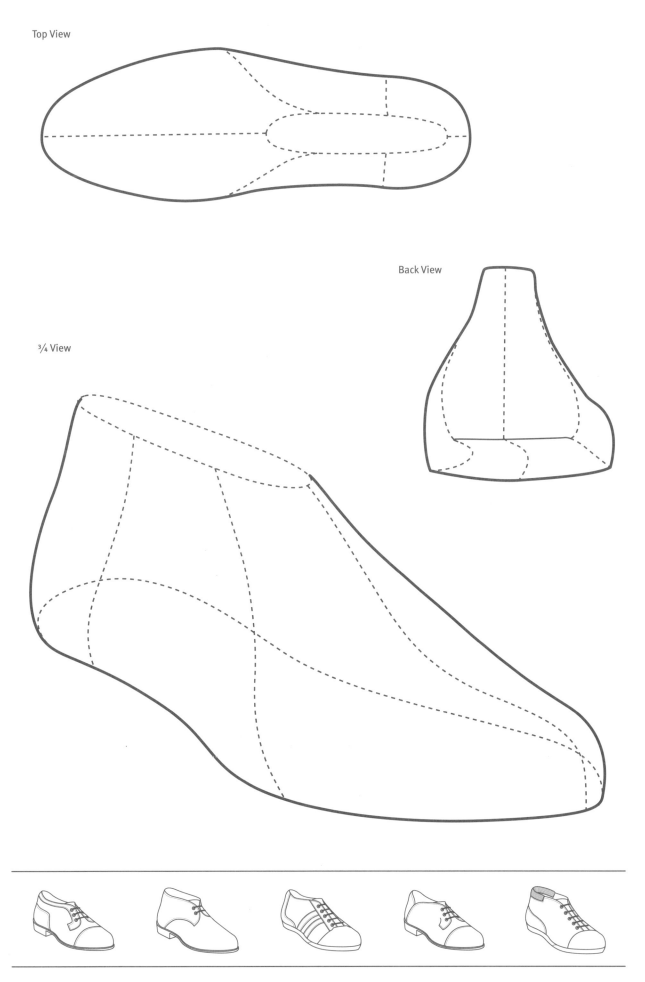

MEN'S CHISEL TOE LAST TEMPLATES

Side View

Side View

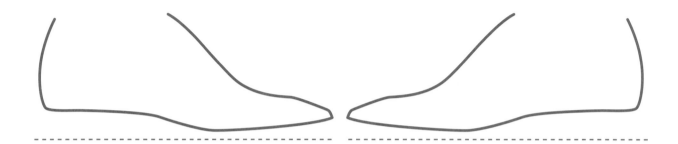

Side View

EXAMPLES

Top View

Back View

¾ View

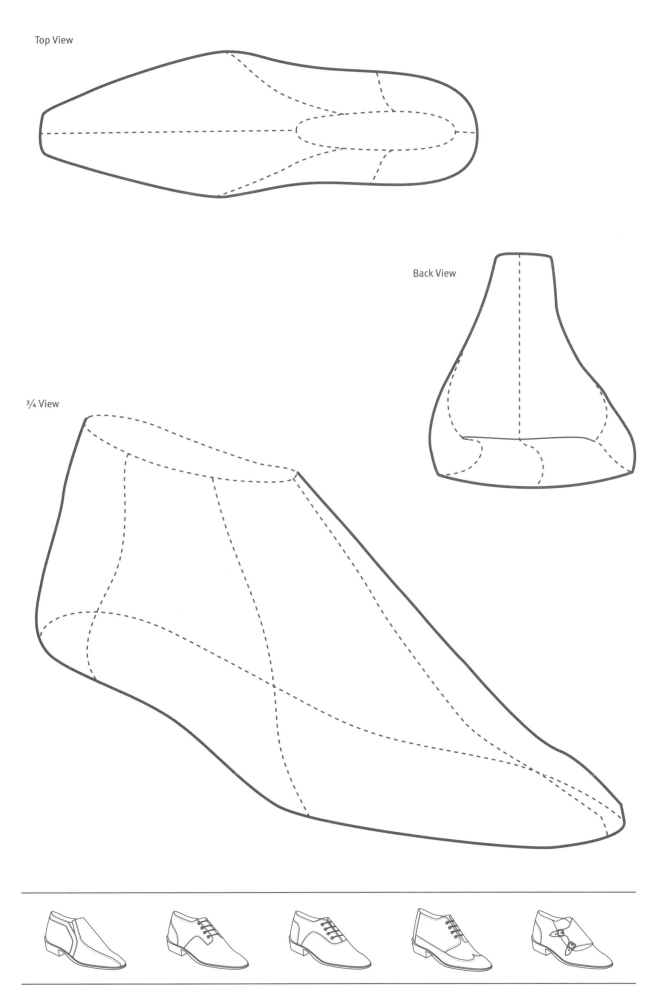

BOOT LAST TEMPLATES

Side View   Side View

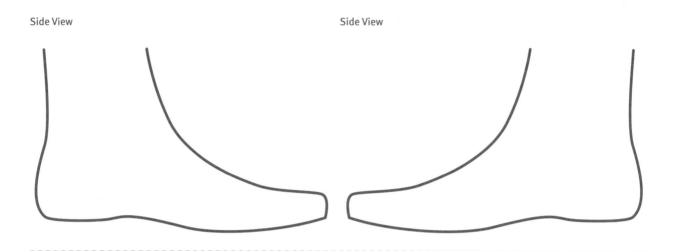

Side View

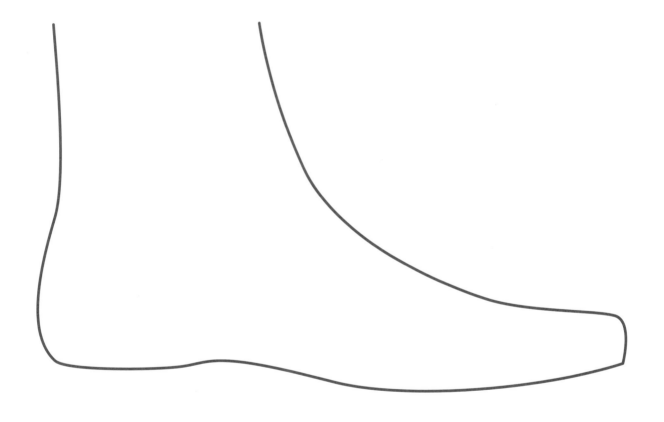

EXAMPLES

Top View

¾ View

Back View

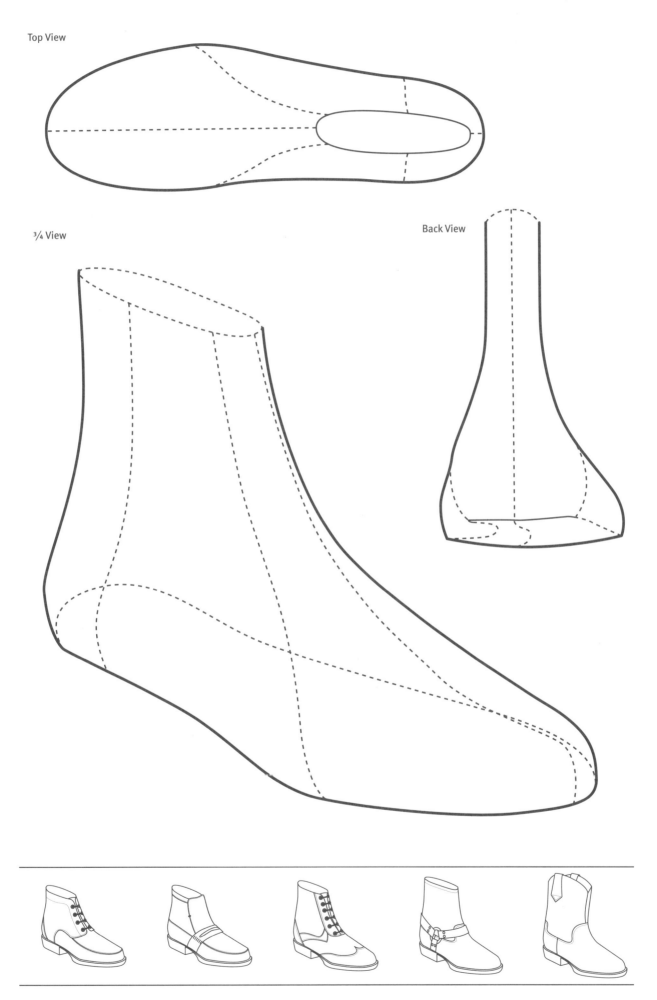

ATHLETIC SHOE LAST TEMPLATES

Side View

Side View

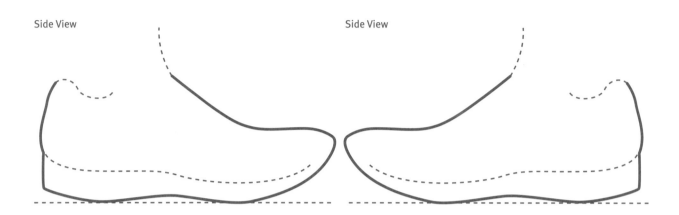

Side View

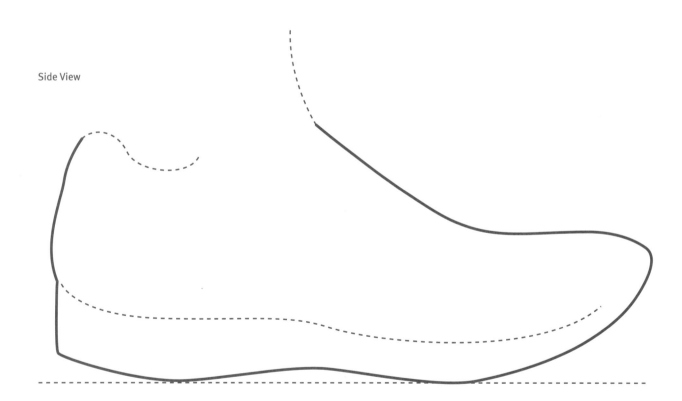

EXAMPLES

Top View

Bottom View

Back View

¾ View

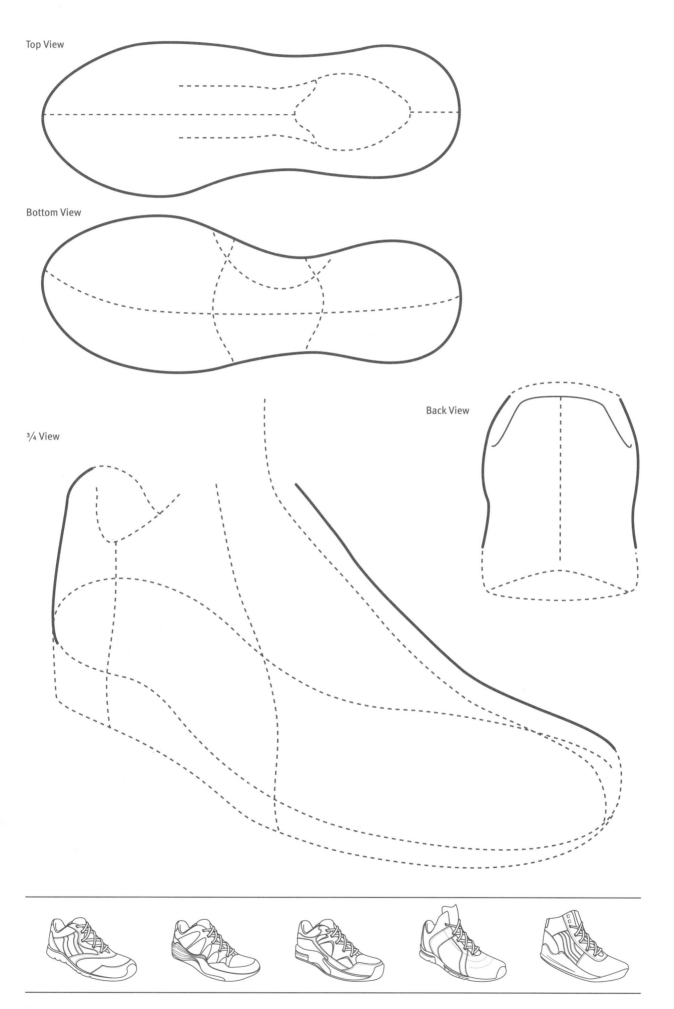

PART VIII

SHOE
TEMPLATES

Ballet Flat
P.80

Folding Ballet Flat
P.81

Espadrille
P.82

Slip-on
P.83

Mary Jane Flat
P.84

Clog
P.85

Evening Slipper
P.86

Opera Pump
P.87

Boat Shoe
P.88

Wallabee
P.89

Slip-on Loafer
P.90

Penny Loafer
P.91

Kiltie Tassel Loafer
P.92

Oxford
P.93

Derby
P.94

Blucher
P.95

Whole Cut Oxford
P.96

Ankle Strap Sandal
P.97

Slingback Thong
P.98

Huarache
P.99

Gladiator Sandal
P.100

Mule Sandal
P.101

Ghillie Sandal
P.102

1" Pump
P.103

2" Pump
P.104

3" Pump
P.105

4" Pump
P.106

5" Pump
P.107

Round-toe Pump
P.108

Pointy Pump
P.109

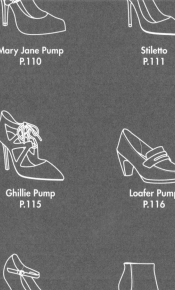

Mary Jane Pump
P.110

Stiletto
P.111

Slingback
P.112

T-bar Pump
P.113

Peep Toe
P.114

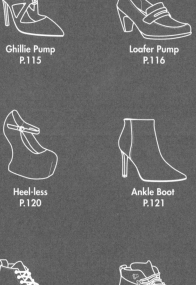

Ghillie Pump
P.115

Loafer Pump
P.116

Platform
P.117

Wedge
P.118

Oxford Pump
P.119

Heel-less
P.120

Ankle Boot
P.121

Chukka
P.122

Chelsea Boot
P.123

Dress Boot
P.124

Duck Boot
P.125

Hiking Boot
P.126

Jodhpur Boot
P.127

Pecos Boot
P.128

Logger Boot
P.129

UGG Boot
P.130

Cowboy Boot
P.131

Slouch Boot
P.132

Vans Slip-on
P.133

Low-top Converse
P.134

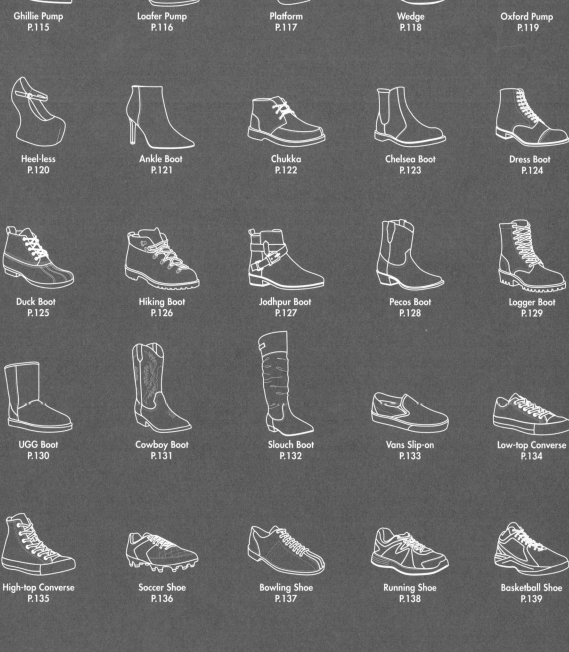

High-top Converse
P.135

Soccer Shoe
P.136

Bowling Shoe
P.137

Running Shoe
P.138

Basketball Shoe
P.139

BALLET FLAT

Ballet flats are derived from women's soft ballet slippers, with a very thin heel or without a heel.

Top View

3/4 View

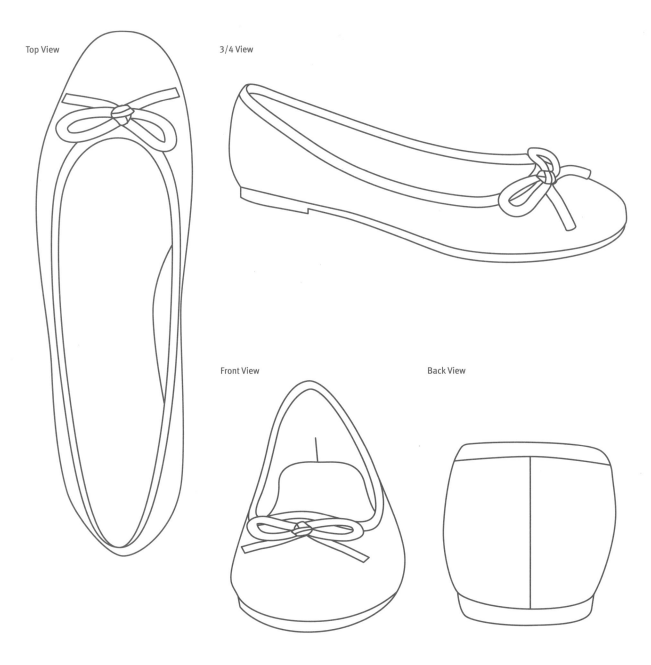

Front View

Back View

Side View

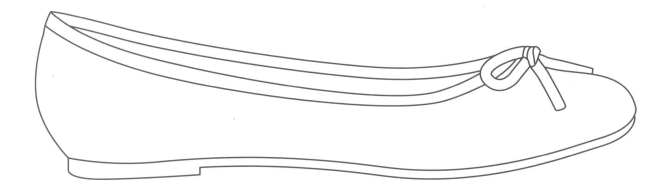

FOLDING BALLET FLAT

Similar to ballet flats but an elastic trim is added along the topline.

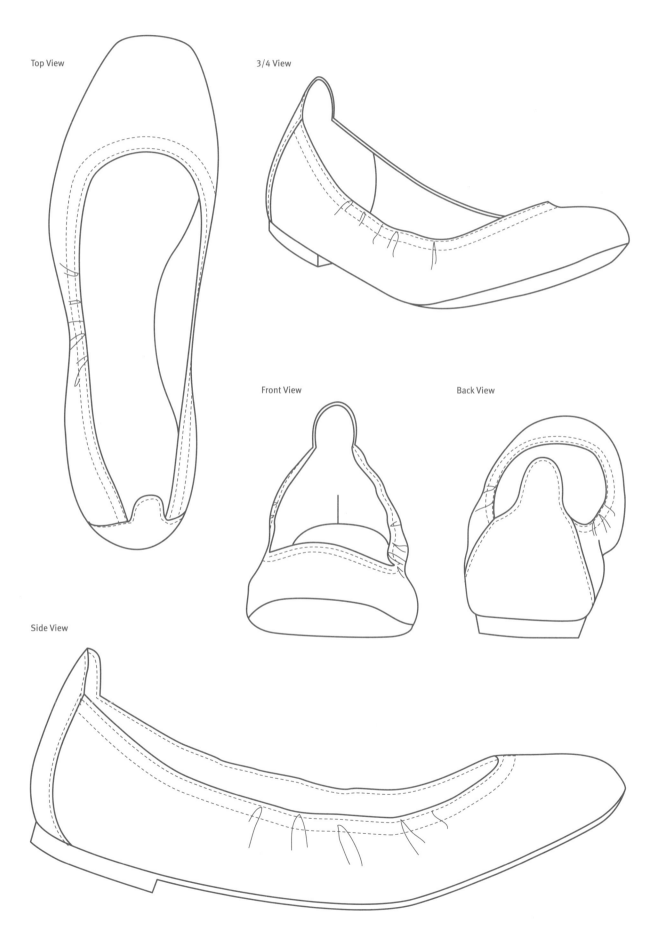

Top View

3/4 View

Front View

Back View

Side View

ESPADRILLE

The uppers vary widely in style, and usually have a canvas or cotton fabric upper and a flexible sole made of jute rope. The jute rope sole is the defining characteristic of an espadrille.

Top View

3/4 View

Front View

Back View

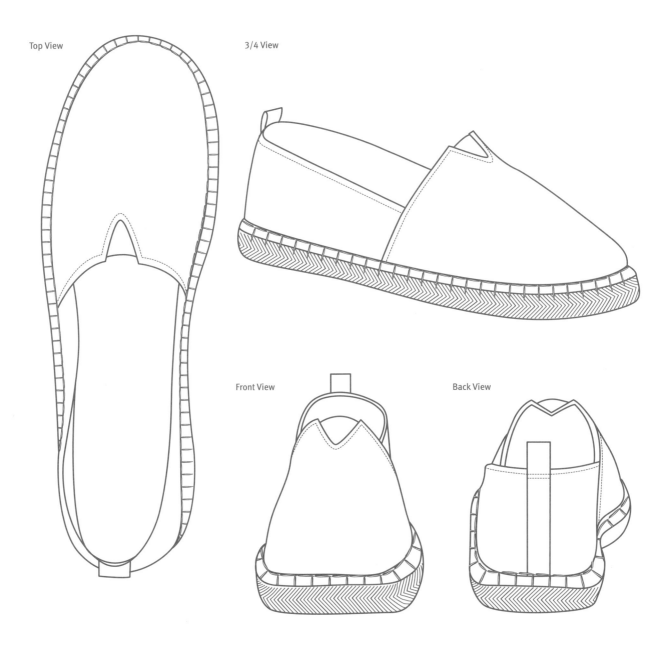

Side View

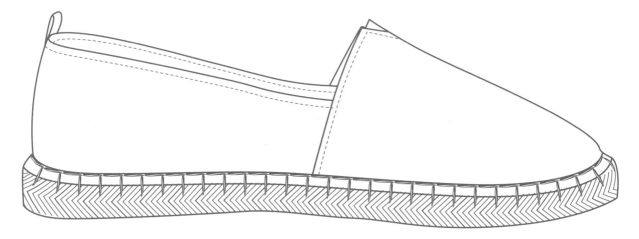

SLIP-ON

Slip-ons are typically low, lace-less shoes.

Top View

3/4 View

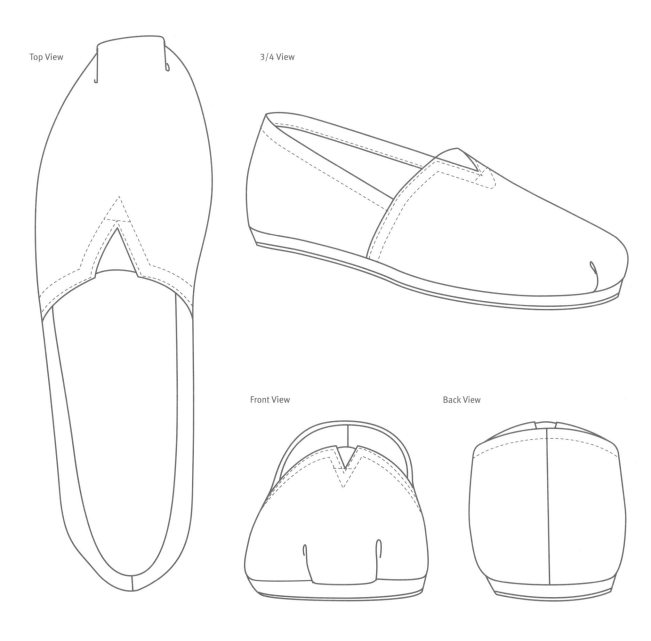

Front View

Back View

Side View

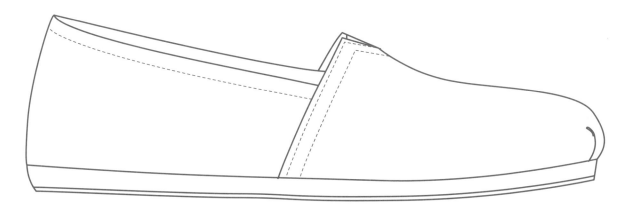

MARY JANE FLAT

Mary Janes is the American term for closed, low-cut shoes with one or more straps across the top.

Top View

3/4 View

Front View

Back View

Side View

CLOG

Clogs are a type of footwear which are made partly or completely from wood traditionally. They usually have a round big toe and no fastening.

Top View

3/4 View

Front View

Back View

Side View

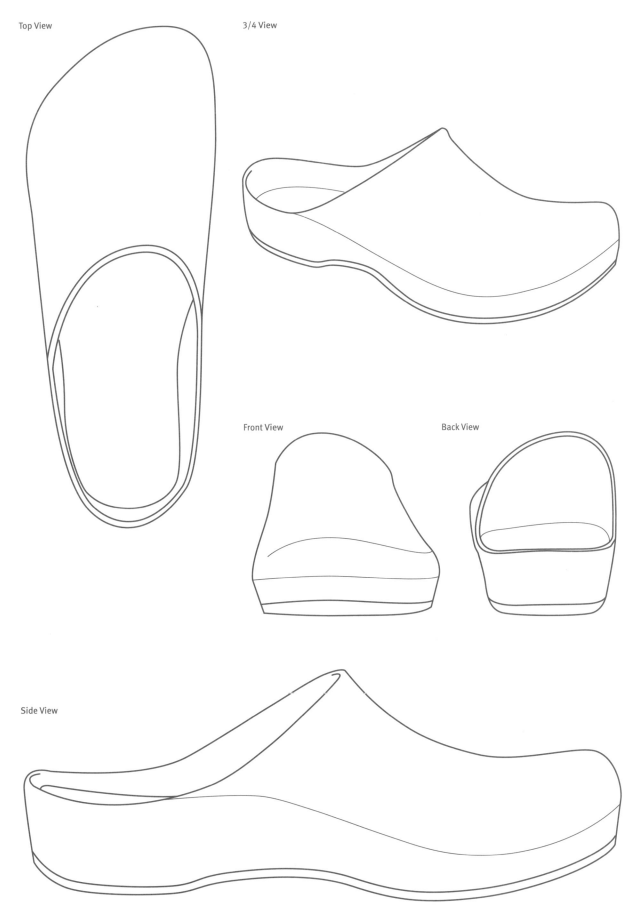

EVENING SLIPPER

Also known as Prince Albert slippers, evening slippers are always made of velvet and have leather soles.

Top View

3/4 View

Front View

Back View

Side View

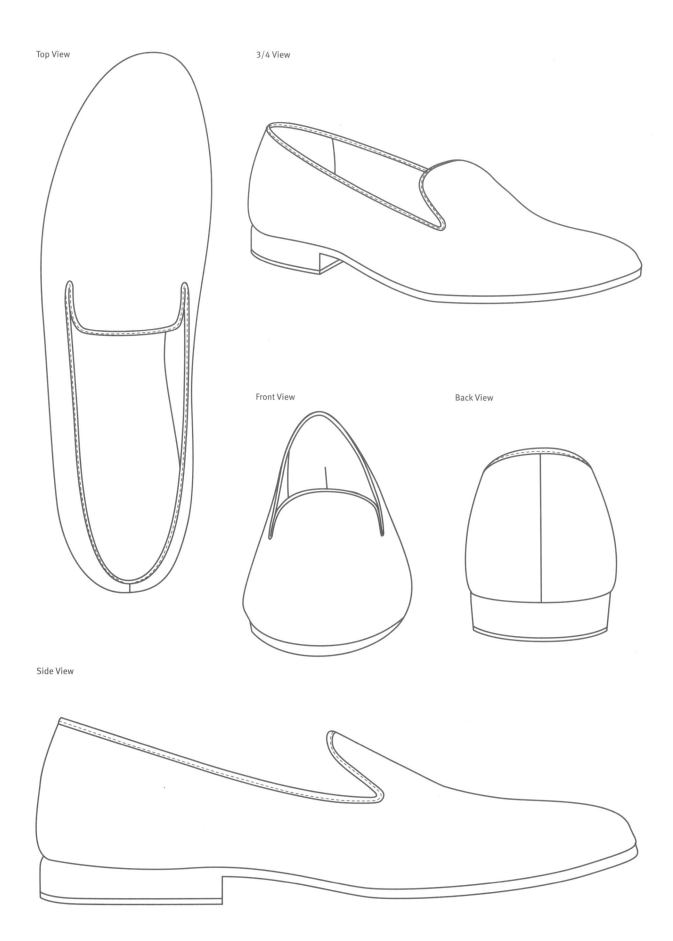

OPERA PUMP

Also known as court shoes, opera pumps are always with a low-cut front and without fastenings. They are worn by men and women traditionally in formal occasions during the Victorian Times.

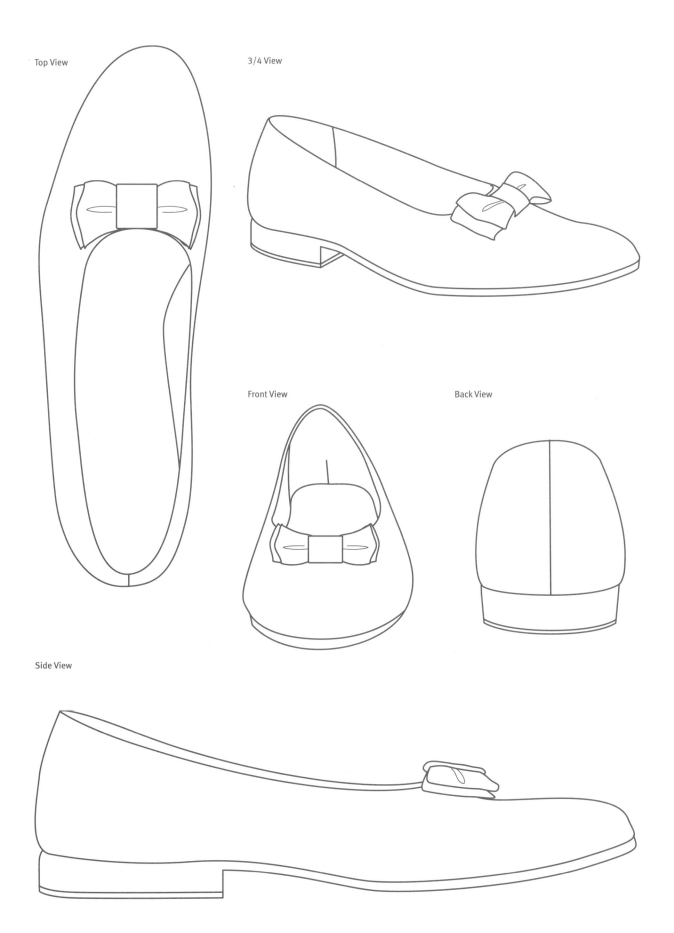

Top View

3/4 View

Front View

Back View

Side View

BOAT SHOE

Boat shoes (also known as deck shoes or topsiders) are typically made of canvas or leather with non-marking rubber soles designed for use on boats.

Top View

3/4 View

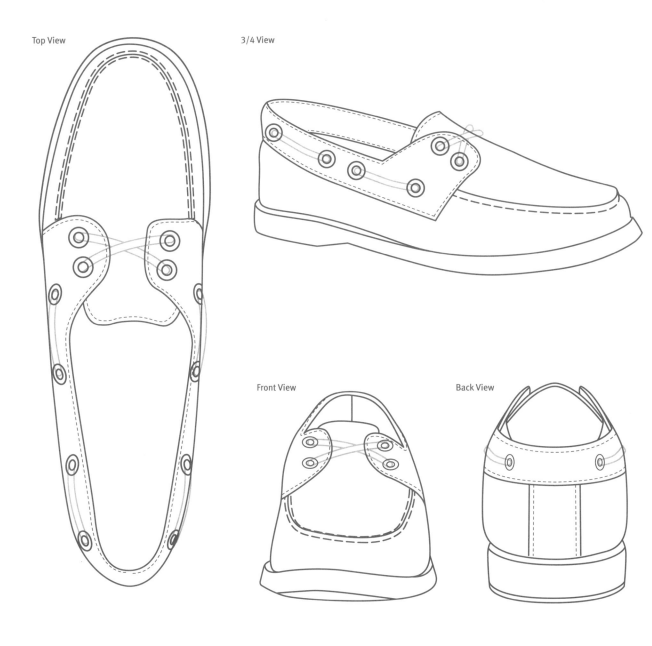

Front View

Back View

Side View

WALLABEE

Wallabees have been produced by Clarks shoes since 1967 and they come in shoe and in boot styles. Both are made out of two pieces of leather or suede in the classic moccasin style, two eyelets and a wedge sole.

Top View

3/4 View

Front View

Back View

Side View

SLIP-ON LOAFER

Slip-on loafers are typically low, lace-less shoes. They are always worn with city lounge suits in America.

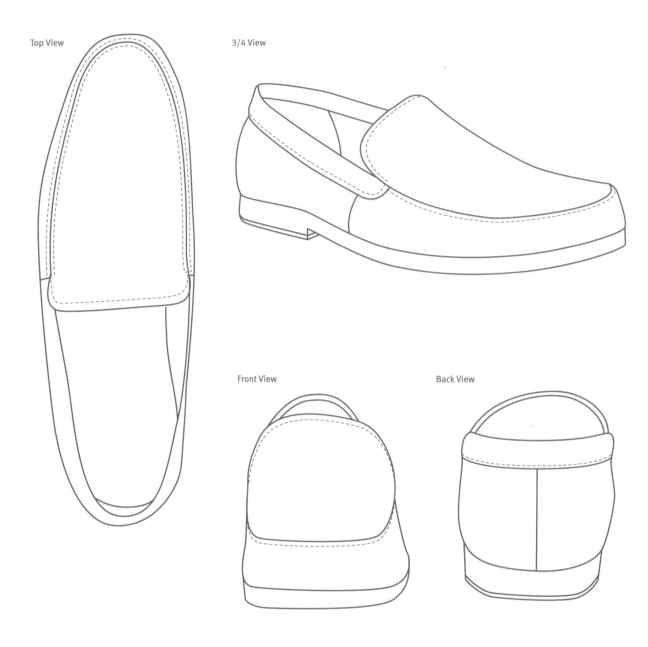

Top View

3/4 View

Front View

Back View

Side View

PENNY LOAFER

Penny loafers are a type of slip-on shoes, while the term penny loafer has uncertain beginnings. One explanation is that two pennies could be slipped into the slit, enough money to make an emergency phone call in the 1930s.

Top View

3/4 View

Front View

Back View

Side View

KILTIE TASSEL LOAFER

Kiltie tassel loafers are a type of slip-on loafers which were first introduced as "Aurlandskoen" in Norway. They often feature tassel on the fronts, or metal decorations.

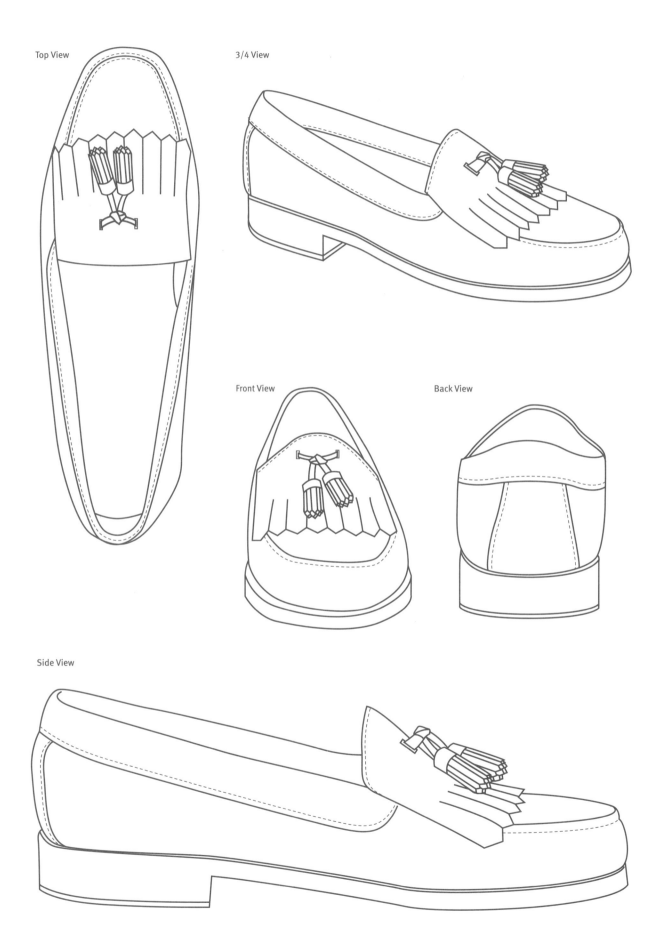

Top View

3/4 View

Front View

Back View

Side View

OXFORD

Oxford shoes are characterized by shoelace eyelet tabs that are attached under the vamp, a feature termed "closed lacing". Oxfords are the standard shoes to wear with most suits.

Top View

3/4 View

Front View

Back View

Side View

DERBY

Derby shoes are a type of shoes characterized by shoelace eyelet tabs that are sewn on top of a single-piece vamp. This construction method, also known as "open lacing", contrasts with the Oxfords.

Top View

3/4 View

Front View

Back View

Side View

BLUCHER

Blucher shoes also feature "open lacing", but they are made from a single piece of leather, while Derby shoes are typically made from 3 pieces of leather.

Top View

3/4 View

Back View

Side View

Front View

WHOLE CUT OXFORD

Instead of multiple pieces of leather being stitched together to make the upper, whole cut Oxfords are cut from just one piece as a hyper-clean look.

Top View

3/4 View

Front View

Back View

Side View

ANKLE STRAP SANDAL

Ankle strap sandals are a type of sandals with a buckled strap around the ankle.

Top View

3/4 View

Front View

Back View

Side View

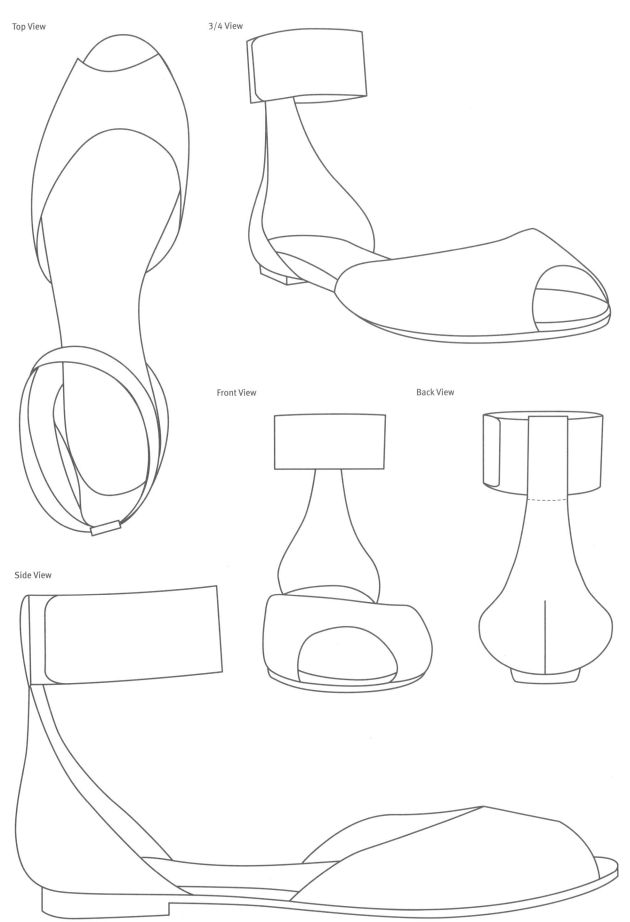

SLINGBACK THONG

Slingback thongs are characterized by a strap that crosses the heel or ankle.

Top View

3/4 View

Front View

Back View

Side View

HUARACHE

Huaraches are a type of Mexican sandals. They have a woven-leather form in the upper.

Top View

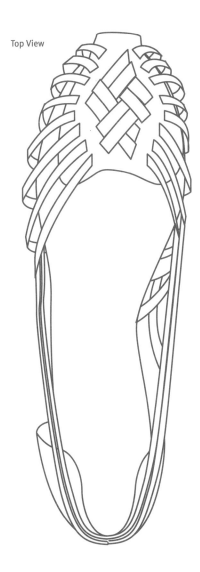

3/4 View

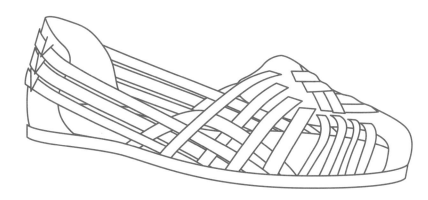

Front View

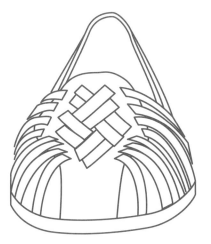

Back View

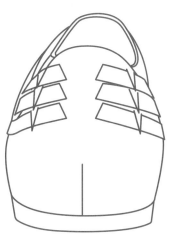

Side View

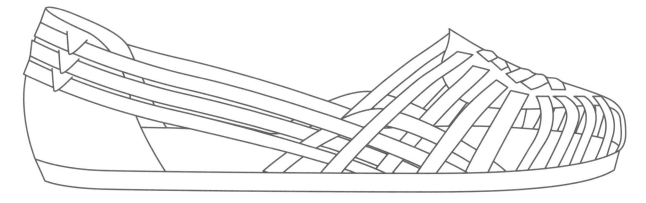

GLADIATOR SANDAL

Gladiator sandals are T-strap sandals with several straps running across the front of the foot. These sandals were favored by Ancient Greeks and Romans.

Top View

3/4 View

Front View

Back View

Side View

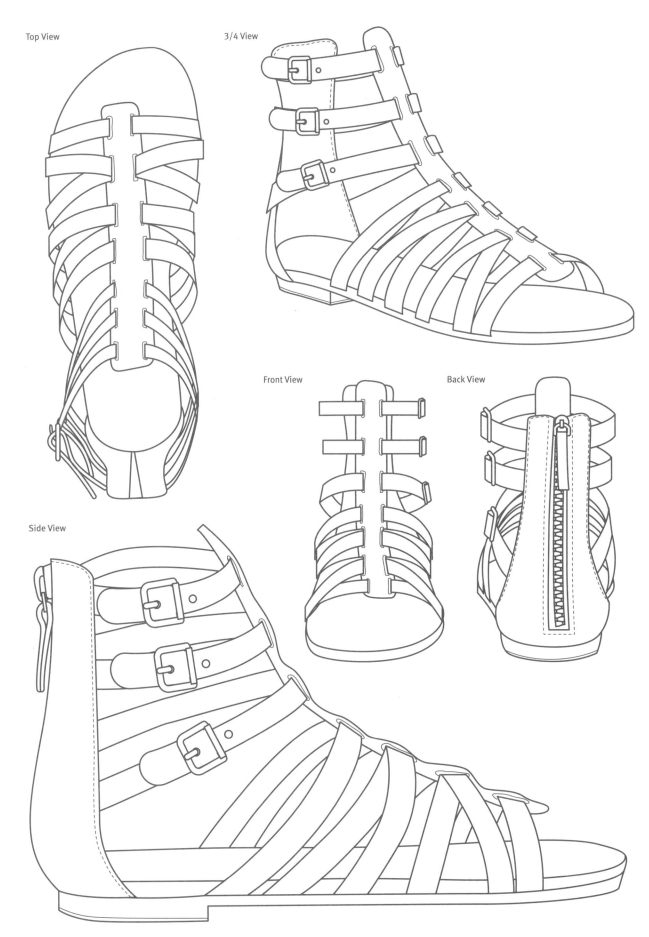

MULE SANDAL

Mule sandals have no back which allow the feet to just slide into them.

Top View

3/4 View

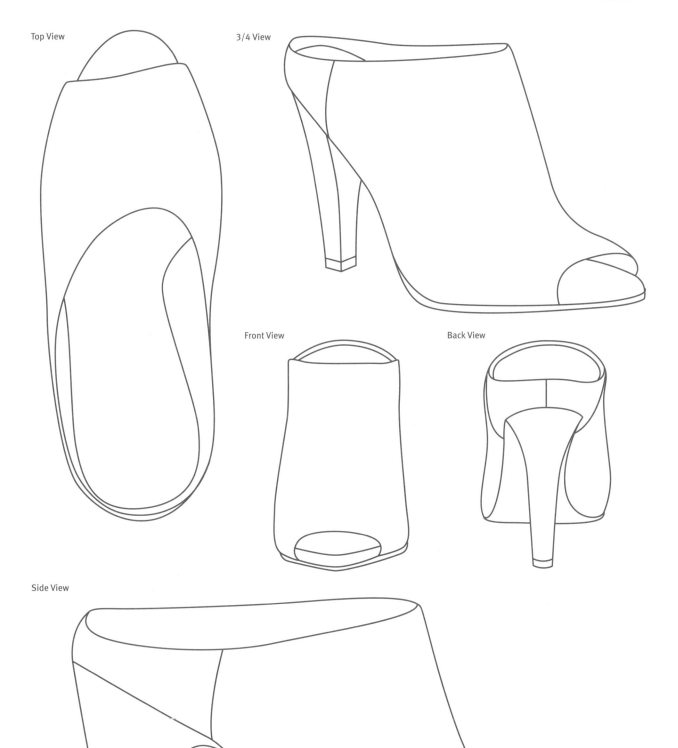

Front View

Back View

Side View

GHILLIE SANDAL

Ghilles were originally worn by people in Ireland when they were dancing. They use laces which criss-cross the top of the foot and are tied together similar to a sneaker.

Top View

3/4 View

Front View

Back View

Side View

1" PUMP

Pumps, or court shoes, are shoes with a low-cut front and usually without a fastening. A 1" pump is considered as a "low heel".

Top View

3/4 View

Front View

Back View

Side View

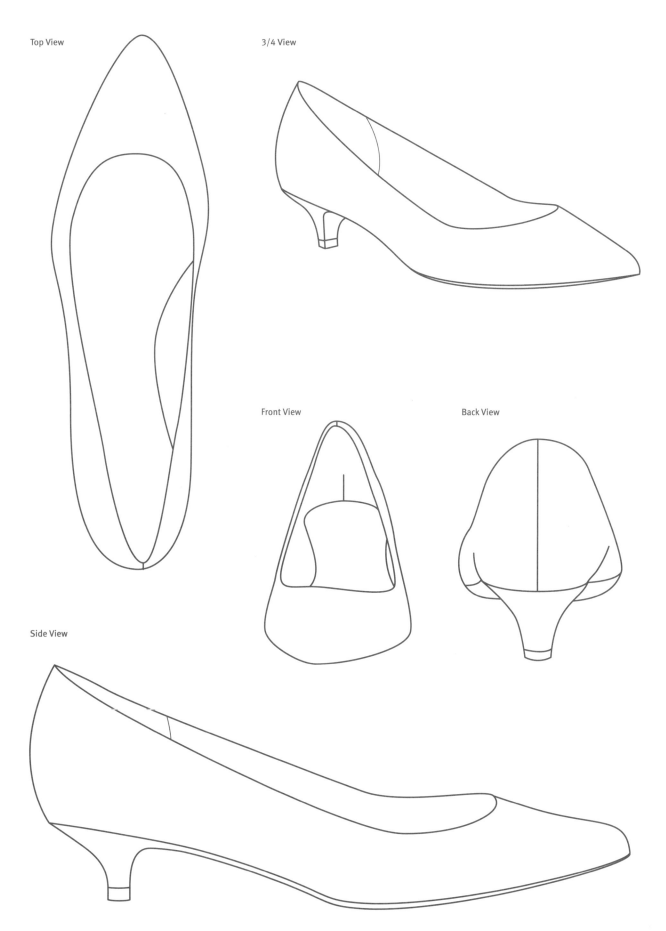

2" PUMP

Pumps, or court shoes, are shoes with a low-cut front and usually without a fastening. A 2" pump is considered as a "low heel".

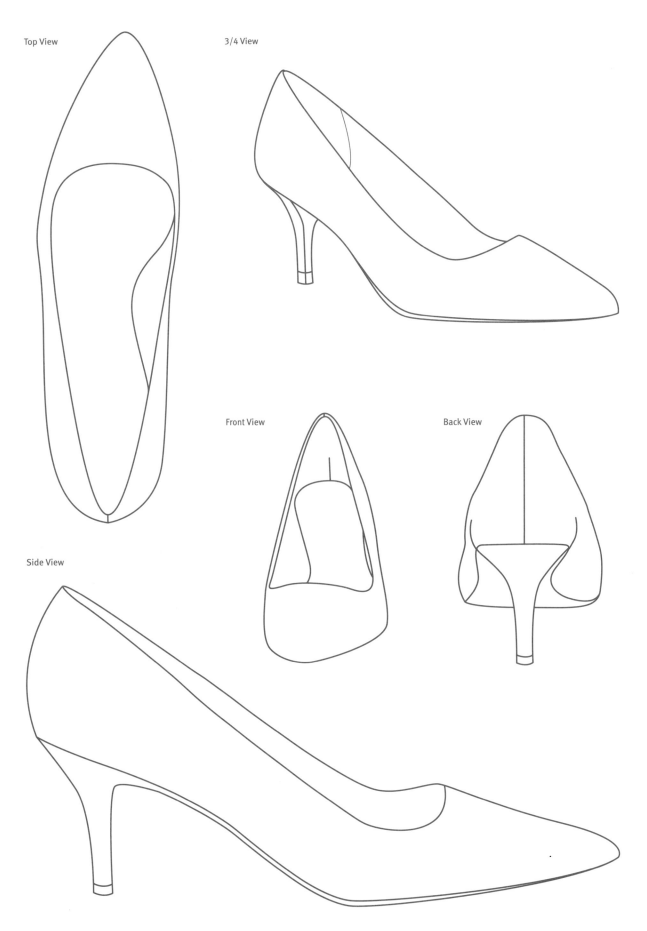

Top View

3/4 View

Front View

Back View

Side View

3" PUMP

Pumps, or court shoes, are shoes with a low-cut front and usually without a fastening. A 3" pump is considered as a "mid heel".

Top View

3/4 View

Front View

Back View

Side View

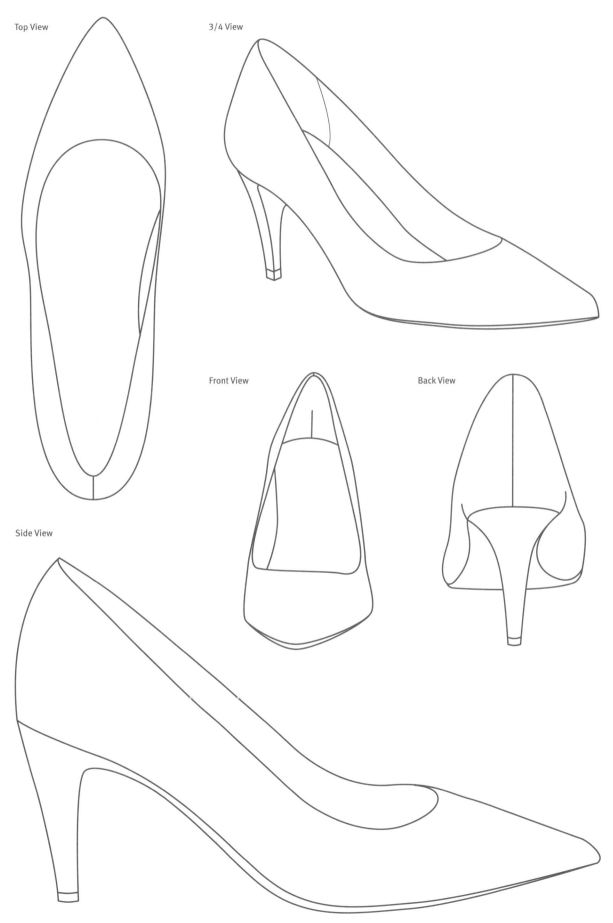

4" PUMP

Pumps, or court shoes, are shoes with a low-cut front and usually without a fastening. A 4" pump is considered as a "mid heel".

Top View

3/4 View

Front View

Back View

Side View

5" PUMP

Pumps, or court shoes, are shoes with a low-cut front and usually without a fastening. A 5" pump is considered as a "high heel".

Top View

3/4 View

Front View

Back View

Side View

ROUND-TOE PUMP

Round-toe pumps are a type of pumps with a rounded toe.

Top View

3/4 View

Front View

Back View

Side View

POINTY PUMP

Pointy pumps are a type of pumps with a pointed toe.

Top View

3/4 View

Front View

Back View

Side View

MARY JANE PUMP

Mary Jane is an American term for closed, low-cut shoes with one or more straps on the top.

Top View

3/4 View

Front View

Back View

Side View

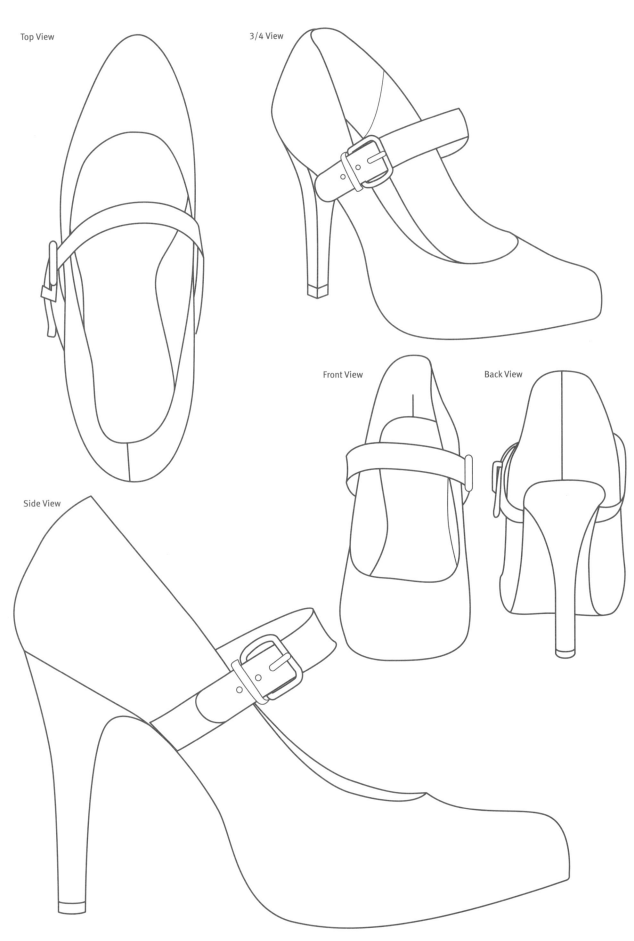

STILETTO

Stiletto heels are long, thin, high heels found on some boots and shoes, usually for women.

Top View

3/4 View

Front View

Back View

Side View

SLINGBACK

Slingbacks have a strap that crosses the heel or ankle.

Top View

3/4 View

Front View

Back View

Side View

T-BAR PUMP

They are closed, low-cut shoes with two or more straps forming a T-shape. There is one or more straps across the instep passing through a perpendicular, central strap that extends from the vamp.

Top View

3/4 View

Front View

Back View

Side View

PEEP TOE

Peep-toe shoes are women's shoes in which there is an opening at the toe box which allows the toes to show.

Top View

3/4 View

Front View

Back View

Side View

GHILLIE PUMP

Ghilles were originally worn by people in Ireland when they were dancing. Laces are used which criss-cross the top of the foot and are tied together similar to a sneaker.

Top View

3/4 View

Front View

Back View

Side View

LOAFER PUMP

They are a type of pumps with the upper similar to loafers.

Top View

3/4 View

Front View

Back View

Side View

PLATFORM

Platform shoes are shoes, boots, or sandals with thick soles.
They are often made of cork, plastic, rubber, or wood.

Top View

3/4 View

Front View

Side View

Back View

WEDGE

Wedges are shoes or boots with a sole in the form of a wedge so
that one piece of material serves as both the sole and the heel.

Top View

3/4 View

Front View

Back View

Side View

OXFORD PUMP

Oxford pumps are a combination of high-heeled pumps and Oxford shoes. The features of Oxford shoes, e.g. closed lacing & punch row, could be found on Oxford pumps.

Top View

3/4 View

Front View

Back View

Side View

HEEL-LESS

Heel-less shoes are a type of high-heeled shoes, with no heels.
Wearers have to put the weight on the toe instead of the heel
when walking.

Top View

3/4 View

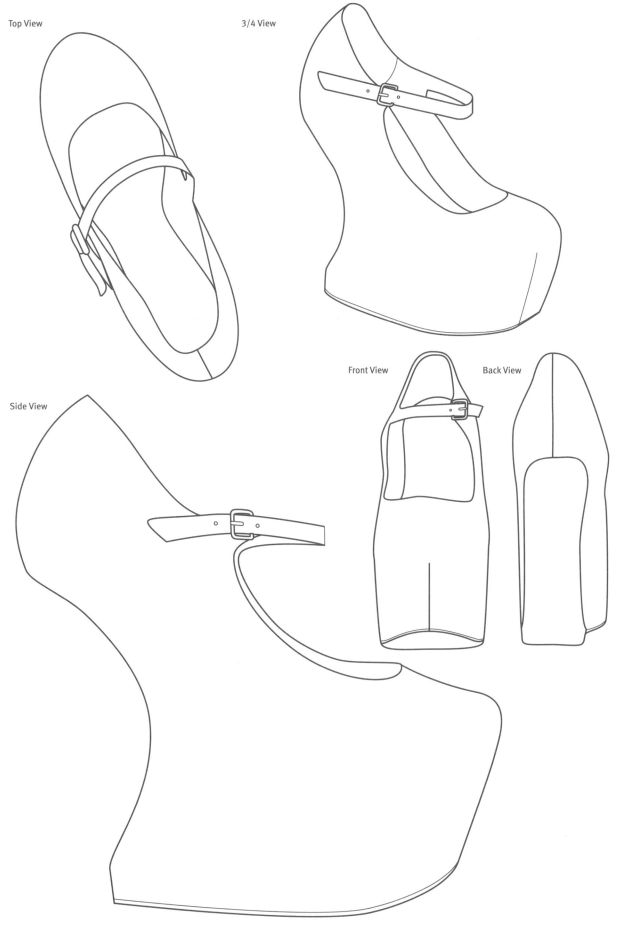

Side View

Front View

Back View

ANKLE BOOT

Ankle boots are ankle high while the shaft of the boot is absent.

Top View

3/4 View

Front View

Back View

Side View

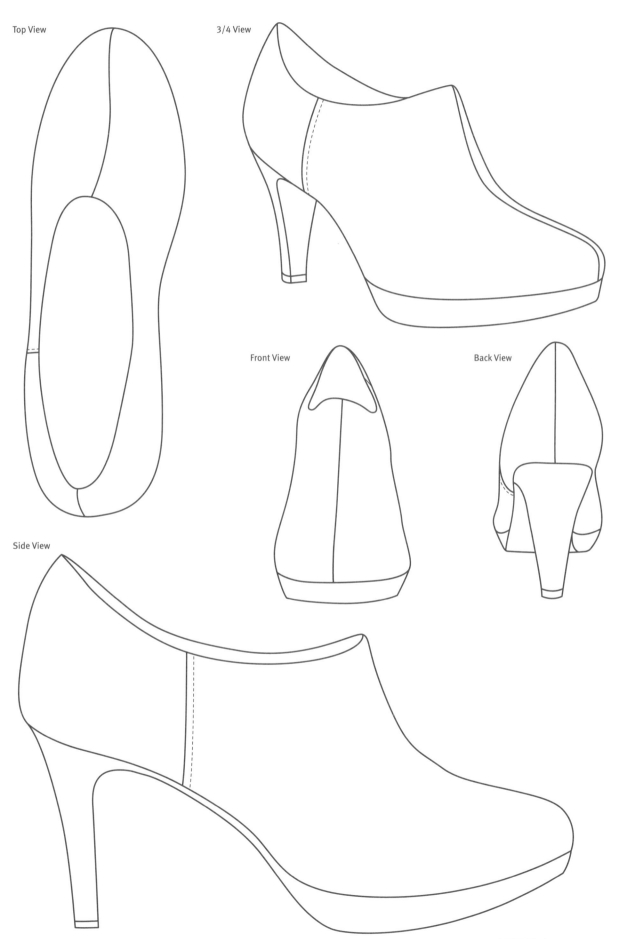

CHUKKA

Chukka boots are ankle-length boots with two or three pairs of eyelets for lacing. They are usually made from calfskin or suede.

Top View

3/4 View

Front View

Back View

Side View

CHELSEA BOOT

Chelsea boots are close-fitting, ankle-high boots. There is a elastic side panel, enabling it to be slipped on and off.

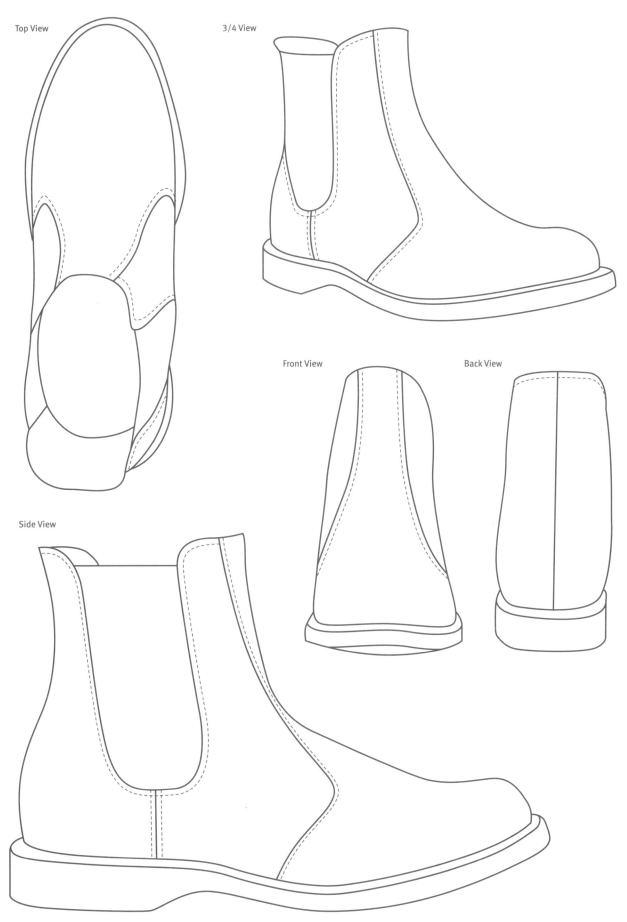

Top View

3/4 View

Front View

Back View

Side View

DRESS BOOT

Dress boots are short leather boots worn by men. They are similar to dress shoes, but with uppers covering the ankles.

Top View

3/4 View

Front View

Back View

Side View

DUCK BOOT

Designed In 1912, duck boots were created as waterproof boots that were sold to hunters. The boots are made of waterproof lightweight leather uppers and rubber bottoms.

Top View

3/4 View

Front View

Back View

Side View

HIKING BOOT

Hiking boots are constructed to provide comfort for walking considerable distance over rough terrain, and protect the hiker's feet against water, mud, rocks, etc.

Top View

3/4 View

Front View

Back View

Side View

JODHPUR BOOT

Fastened with a strap and buckle, jodhpur boots are ankle boots designed as riding boots with a rounded toe and a low heel.

Top View

3/4 View

Front View

Back View

Side View

PECOS BOOT

Pecos boots were introduced in 1953 and were durable and practical, combining the western style with the ruggedness of work boots. There are ears on both sides of the boots.

Top View

3/4 View

Front View

Back View

Side View

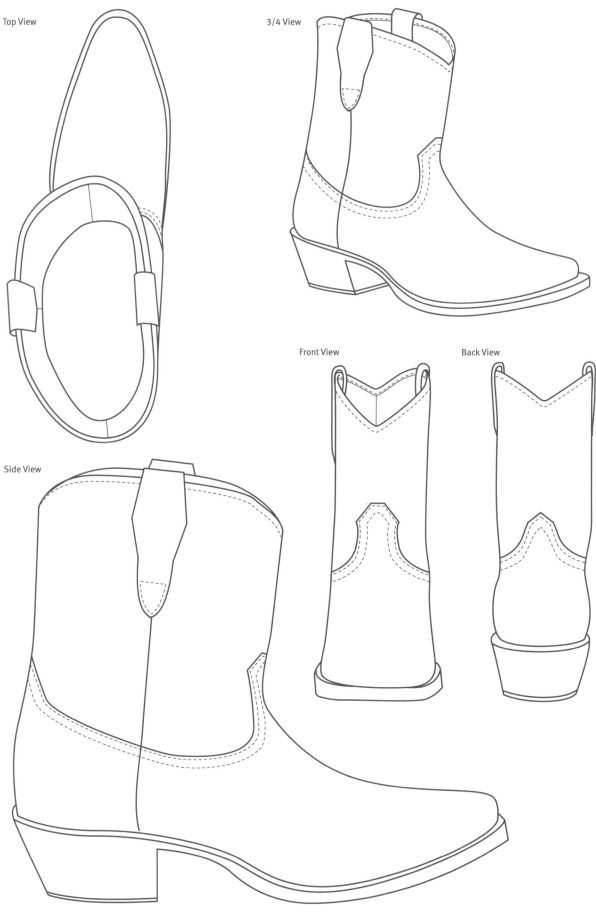

LOGGER BOOT

Also named caulk boots, logger boots are a type of working leather nail-soled boots worn by loggers traditionally.

Top View

3/4 View

Side View

Front View

Back View

UGG BOOT

UGG boots are known in Australia and New Zealand as a unisex style of sheepskin boots. They are typically made of twin-faced sheepskin with fleece inside, a tanned outer surface and a synthetic sole.

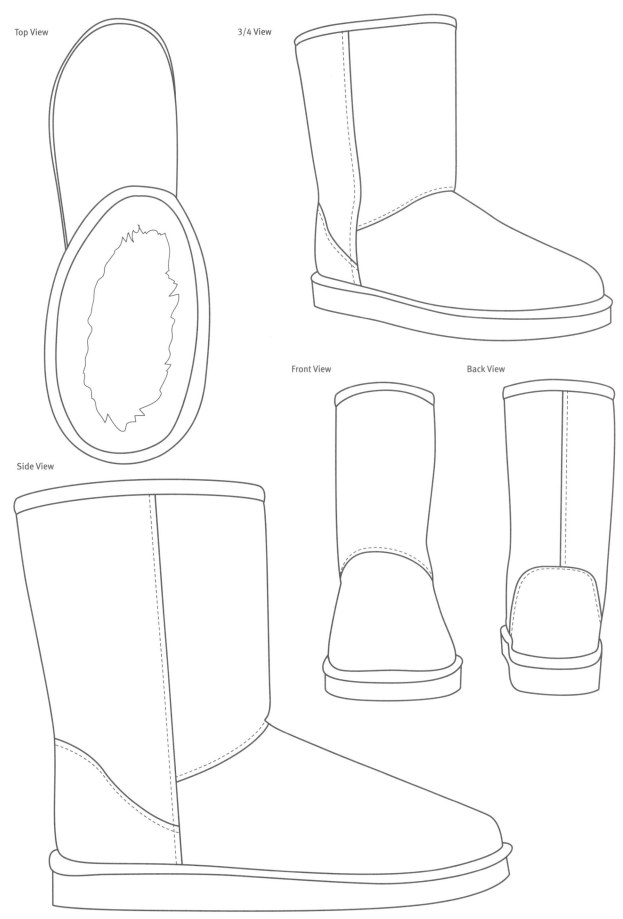

Top View

3/4 View

Side View

Front View

Back View

COWBOY BOOT

Cowboy boots refer to a specific style of riding boots, historically worn by cowboys. They have a Cuban heel, rounded to pointed toe, high shaft, and traditionally, no lacing.

Top View

3/4 View

Side View

Front View

Back View

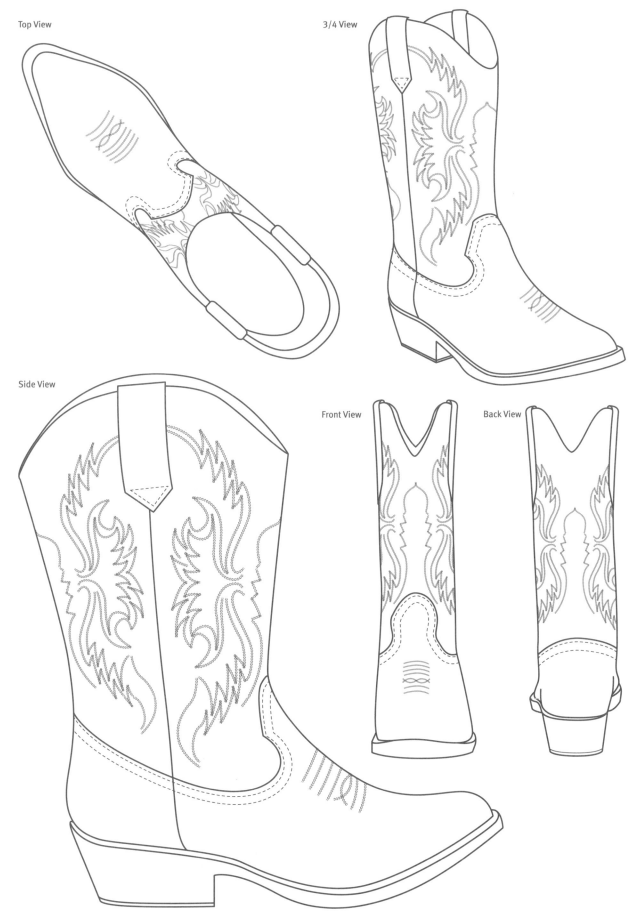

SLOUCH BOOT

Slouch boots are a type of shoes with a flexible boot shaft that rumples instead of standing upright. They are typically loose around the legs and can be as short as ankle length or as tall as over-the-knee.

Top View

3/4 View

Side View

Front View

Back View

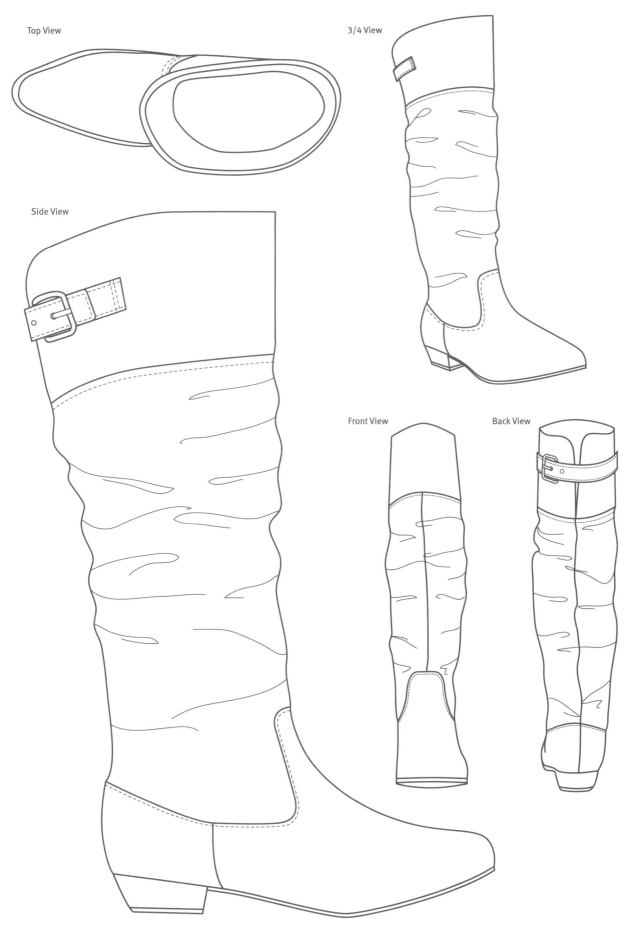

VANS SLIP-ON

Vans slip-ons are typically low, lace-less shoes. There are elasticated inserts on the sides which allow the shoes to be easily removed but remain snug when worn.

Top View

3/4 View

Front View

Back View

Side View

LOW-TOP CONVERSE

With the same features of its high-top version, the low-cut version was designed in 1957 and is still manufacturing today.

Top View

3/4 View

Front View

Back View

Side View

HIGH-TOP CONVERSE

Designed In 1917, the shoes are composed of a rubber sole and canvas upper and were designed to be elite shoes for the professional basketball league.

Top View

3/4 View

Front View

Back View

Side View

SOCCER SHOE

They are football boots which are called soccer shoes in North America. There are studs on the outsole of the shoes which can aid grip when running on grass.

Top View

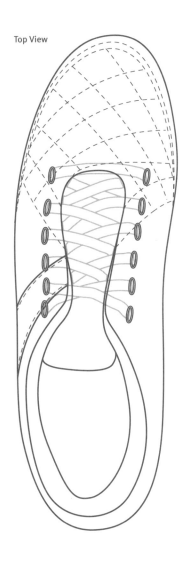

3/4 View

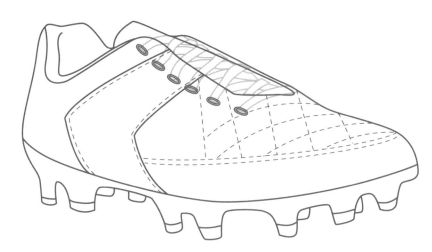

Front View

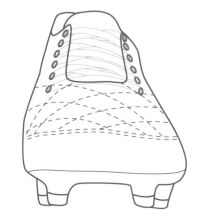

Back View

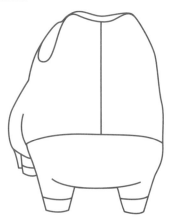

Side View

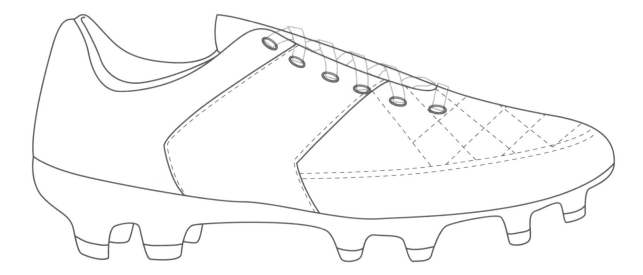

BOWLING SHOE

Each shoe in a pair of performance bowling shoes serves a different purpose. One bowling shoe is for sliding, and the other is for braking.

Top View

3/4 View

Front View

Back View

Side View

RUNNING SHOE

There are different types of running shoes in the market, e.g. road running shoes and trail running shoes, while different features are added to improve the running experience.

Top View

3/4 View

Front View

Back View

Side View

BASKETBALL SHOE

They are a type of athletic footwear designed for playing basketball. They come in a variety of materials, designs, and even ankle heights, providing many options for different playing needs.

Top View

3/4 View

Front View

Back View

Side View

WOMEN'S SHOE INTERNATIONAL SIZE CHART

US/Canada	5	5½	6	6½	7	7½	8	8½	9	9½	10	10½	12	13	14	15½
UK	2½	3	3½	4	4½	5	5½	6	6½	7	7½	8	9½	10½	11½	13
Euro	35	35½	36	37	37½	38	38½	39	40	41	42	43	44	45	46½	48½
Australia/NZ	3½	4	4½	5	5½	6	6½	7	7½	8	8½	9	10½	11½	12½	14
Japan	21	21.5	22	22.5	23	23.5	24	24.5	25	25.5	26	27	28	29	30	31
China	35.5	36	37	37.5	38	39	39.5	40	41	41.5	42	43	44.5	46	47	48
Mexico	-	-	-	-	-	4.5	5	5.5	6	6.5	7	7.5	9	10	11	12.5
Korea	228	231	235	238	241	245	248	251	254	257	260	267	273	279	286	292
Modopoint	228	231	235	238	241	245	248	251	254	257	260	267	273	279	286	292

MEN'S SHOE INTERNATIONAL SIZE CHART

US/Canada	4½	5	5½	6	6½	7	7½	8	8½	9	9½	10	10½	11	11½	12	12½	13
UK	4	4½	5	5½	6	6½	7	7½	8	8½	9	9½	10	10½	11	11½	12	12½
Euro	36	37	37½	38	38½	39	40	41	42	43	43½	44	44½	45	45½	46	46½	47
Australia/NZ	4	4½	5	5½	6	6½	7	7½	8	8½	9	9½	10	10½	11	11½	12	12½
Japan	22.5	23	23.5	24	24.5	25	25.5	26	26.5	27	27.5	28	28.5	29	29.5	30	30.5	31
China	37	38	39	39.5	40	41	-	42	43	43.5	44	44.5	45	46	-	47	47.5	48
Mexico	-	4.5	5	5.5	6	6.5	7	7.5	9	-	10	-	11	-	12.5	-	-	-
Korea	235	238	241	245	248	251	254	257	260	263	267	270	273	276	279	283	286	289
Modopoint	235	238	241	245	248	251	254	257	260	263	267	270	273	276	279	283	286	289

KID'S SHOE INTERNATIONAL SIZE CHART (AGE 0-4)

US/Canada	½	1	1½	2	2½	3	3½	4	4½	5	5½	6	6½	7	7½
UK	0	½	1	1	1½	2	2½	3	3½	4	4½	5	5½	6	6½
Euro	15½	16	16½	17	17½	18	18½	19	19½	20	21	22	22½	23	23½
Australia/NZ	0	½	1	1	1½	2	2½	3	3½	4	4½	5	5½	6	6½

KID'S SHOE INTERNATIONAL SIZE CHART (AGE 4-8)

US/Canada	8	8½	9	9½	10	10½	11	11½	12	12½	13	13½	14	14½	15	15½	16
UK	7	7½	8	8½	9	9½	10	10½	11	11½	12	12½	13	13½	14	14½	15
Euro	24	24½	25	26	27	27½	28	29	30	30½	31	31½	32	32½	33	33½	34
Australia/NZ	7	7½	8	8½	9	9½	10	10½	11	11½	12	12½	13	13½	14	14½	15

SHOE WIDTH VARIATION

Womens	Super Slim	Slim	Narrow	Medium	Wide	Extra Wide	Ultra Wide
Mens	Ultra Slim	Super Slim	Slim	Narrow	Medium	Wide	Extra Wide
Symbol	4A	3A	2A, A	B	C, D, E	2E	3E
	AAAA	AAA	AA, A	B	C, D, E	EE	EEE
	SS	S	N	M, R, MW	W, WW	XW	XXW

WOMEN'S SHOE WIDTH

US Women Size	Narrow (N/AA) cm	Medium (M) cm	Wide (W) cm	X-Wide (WW) cm
4	6.7	7.7	8.6	9.6
4.5	6.9	7.9	8.8	9.8
5	7.1	8.1	9	10
5.5	7.3	8.3	9.2	10.2
6	7.5	8.4	9.4	10.3
6.5	7.6	8.6	9.5	10.5
7	7.8	8.7	9.7	10.6
7.5	8	8.9	9.9	10.8
8	8.1	9	10	10.9
8.5	8.3	9.2	10.2	11.1
9	8.4	9.4	10.3	11.3
9.5	8.6	9.5	10.5	11.4
10	8.7	9.7	10.6	11.6
10.5	8.9	9.9	10.8	11.8
11	9	10	10.9	11.9
11.5	9.2	10.2	11.1	12.1
12	9.4	10.3	11.3	12.2

MEN'S SHOE WIDTH

US Men Size	Narrow (C) cm	Medium (D) cm	Wide (E) cm
6	8.4	8.9	9.4
6.5	8.4	9.1	9.7
7	8.6	9.1	9.7
7.5	8.6	9.4	9.9
8	8.9	9.7	9.9
8.5	9.1	9.7	10.2
9	9.1	9.9	10.4
9.5	9.4	9.9	10.4
10	9.7	10.2	10.7
10.5	9.7	10.4	10.9
11	9.9	10.4	10.9
11.5	9.9	10.7	11.2
12	10.2	10.9	11.2
12.5	10.4	10.9	11.4
13	10.4	11.2	11.7
13.5	10.7	11.2	12.2
14	10.7	11.4	12.4